lonely planet

Pocket
EDINBURGH

TOP SIGHTS · LOCAL LIFE · MADE EASY

D0038082

Neil Wilson

In This Book

QuickStart Guide

Your keys to understanding the city – we help you decide what to do and how to do it

Need to Know
Tips for a smooth trip

Neighbourhoods
What's where

Explore Edinburgh

The best things to see and do, neighbourhood by neighbourhood

Top Sights
Make the most of your visit

Local Life
The insider's city

The Best of Edinburgh

The city's highlights in handy lists to help you plan

Best Walks
See the city on foot

Edinburgh's Best...
The best experiences

Survival Guide

Tips and tricks for a seamless, hassle-free city experience

Getting Around
Travel like a local

Essential Information
Including where to stay

Our selection of the city's best places to eat, drink and experience:

◎ **Sights**

⊗ **Eating**

🅑 **Drinking**

✪ **Entertainment**

🅐 **Shopping**

These symbols give you the vital information for each listing:

☎	Telephone Numbers	🚼	Family-Friendly
⊙	Opening Hours	🐾	Pet-Friendly
🅟	Parking	🚌	Bus
⊘	Nonsmoking	🛳	Ferry
@	Internet Access	Ⓜ	Metro
🛜	Wi-Fi Access	Ⓢ	Subway
🥗	Vegetarian Selection	🚊	Tram
🕮	English-Language	🚆	Train

Find each listing quickly on maps for each neighbourhood:

Bar Hemingway

16 🅑 Map p233, B2

Legend has it that Hem self, wielding a machine rate this timber-pan ered bar during showpiece is a n by Papa ar town. Dress s.com; Hôtel Rit ⊙6.30pm-2a

Lonely Planet Pocket Guides are designed to get you straight to the heart of the city.

Inside you'll find all the must-see sights, plus tips to make your visit to each one really memorable. We've split the city into easy-to-navigate neighbourhoods and provided clear maps so you'll find your way around with ease. Our expert authors have searched out the best of the city: walks, food, nightlife and shopping, to name a few. Because you want to explore, our 'Local Life' pages will take you to some of the most exciting areas to experience the real Edinburgh.

And of course you'll find all the practical tips you need for a smooth trip: itineraries for short visits, how to get around, and how much to tip the guy who serves you a drink at the end of a long day's exploration.

It's your guarantee of a really great experience.

Our Promise

You can trust our travel information because Lonely Planet authors visit the places we write about, each and every edition. We never accept freebies for positive coverage, so you can rely on us to tell it like it is.

QuickStart Guide 7

Explore Edinburgh 21

Worth a Trip:

The Best of Edinburgh 125

Edinburgh's Best Walks

Edinburgh's Best ...

Survival Guide 145

QuickStart Guide

Welcome to Edinburgh

Edinburgh is one of Britain's most beautiful cities, with its castle perched upon ancient crags and the medieval maze of the Old Town gazing across verdant gardens to the Georgian elegance of the New Town. History and architecture are leavened with a bacchanalia of bars, innovative restaurants and Scotland's most stylish shops.

Edinburgh city centre
LEONID ANDRONOV/SHUTTERSTOCK ©

Edinburgh Top Sights

Edinburgh Castle (p24)

Attracting more than 1.3 million visitors per year, Edinburgh Castle is Scotland's most popular attraction, a craggy cluster of museums, militaria, chapels, cannons, vaults and prisons, as well as the Scottish Crown Jewels.

Rosslyn Chapel (p122)

Made famous by Dan Brown's *The Da Vinci Code*, this medieval chapel is a symphony in stone, densely decorated with carved symbols and imagery that has been associated with the enigmatic quest for the Holy Grail.

Royal Yacht Britannia (p106)

Since her retirement in 1997, the former floating holiday home of the British royal family has been moored at Leith's Ocean Terminal, offering a fascinating insight into HM the Queen's travels.

Real Mary King's Close (p28)

Sealed off in the 18th century, this buried medieval street was opened to the public in 2003, with atmospheric guided tours of its ancient vaults.

Scottish Parliament Building (p56)

Edinburgh's most spectacular and controversial building, opened in 2004 to house Scotland's devolved parliament, is a confection of strange shapes and symbolic forms.

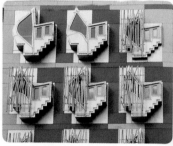

Palace of Holyroodhouse (p54)

The queen's official residence in Scotland has at its heart a tower house that was once home to Mary, Queen of Scots; her bedchamber is the high point of the tour.

National Museum of Scotland (p30)

This museum charts the history of Scotland. Highlights include the Monymusk Reliquary, carried into battle at Bannockburn, and the 12th-century Lewis Chessmen.

Scottish National Portrait Gallery (p66)

This beautifully renovated gallery is now one of the city's top sights, leading visitors entertainingly through Scottish history by means of portraits of famous characters.

Princes Street Gardens (p68)

This dramatically situated city park lines a verdant valley between the spire-spiked skyline of the Old Town and the ordered elegance of the New Town.

JAMES JONES JR/SHUTTERSTOCK ©

SIDDARTH V REDDY/EYEEM/GETTY IMAGES ©

Scottish National Gallery of Modern Art (p86)

Devoted to 20th-century and contemporary art, this gallery is housed in two impressive neoclassical buildings set in gorgeous grounds dotted with sculptures.

Royal Botanic Garden (p96)

These 70 landscaped acres include splendid Victorian glasshouses, colourful swaths of rhododendron and azalea, giant Amazonian water lilies and a famous rock garden.

Edinburgh Local Life

Insider tips to help you find the real city

There's more to Edinburgh than the top tourist sights. Experience a little of what makes the city tick by exploring its hidden backstreets, stylish shops, scenic parkland, and a village within the city.

Explore the Old Town's Hidden History (p34)

▶ Hidden alleys
▶ Historic sites

Much of what makes Edinburgh's Old Town so intriguing is its maze of narrow wynds (alleys) and staircases connecting different levels of the city. Most visitors don't stray from the Royal Mile, but to really appreciate Old Town history you have to delve into the network of hidden alleys.

A Walk Through Holyrood Park (p58)

▶ City-centre scenery
▶ Panoramic views

Holyrood Park, the former hunting ground of Scottish kings, brings a huge chunk of countryside into the heart of the city. Put on your hiking shoes and explore the walking trails that criss-cross its slopes, leading eventually to the picturesque village of Duddingston and its welcoming country pub.

New Town Shopping (p70)

▶ Georgian architecture
▶ Upmarket shops

Once the powerhouse of Edinburgh's financial industry, the New Town's smart Georgian streets have been taken over by a wealth of classy shops and designer outlets. Grab your credit cards and search for that something special in the gorgeous boutiques on Thistle St, before relaxing in one of the city's top lunch spots.

A Sunday Stroll Around Stockbridge (p98)

▶ Unique shops
▶ Stylish street life

Stockbridge began life as a mill village on the Water of Leith, but has long since been swept up in Edinburgh's urban expansion. Enjoy a stroll around one of the city's most desirable districts, home to offbeat boutiques, cute cafes, great neighbourhood bistros and Scotland's best Sunday market.

Cockburn Street, Old Town (p51)
Union Canal (p120)

ALBERT PEGO/GETTY IMAGES ©

WONDERPHOTOS/GETTY IMAGES ©

Other great places to experience the city like a local:

Cockburn Street Shops (p51)

Edinburgh's Mysterious Book Sculptures (p44)

Sandy Bell's (p46)

Urban Hillwalking on Arthur's Seat (p62)

Edinburgh Farmers Market (p90)

Bohemian Broughton (p80)

Cramond Village (p110)

Union Canal (p120)

Southside Brunch (p118)

Edinburgh Zoo (p76)

Edinburgh Day Planner

Day One

Edinburgh Castle (p24) is the city's number one sight, so if you only have a day to spare spend at least the first two hours after opening time here. Take a leisurely stroll down the Royal Mile, stopping off for a prebooked tour of the historic Real Mary King's Close (p28) before having lunch at Wedgwood (p43) or Devil's Advocate (p45).

At the bottom of the Mile, take a one-hour guided tour of the Scottish Parliament Building (p56), before crossing the street to the Palace of Holyroodhouse (p54). Then, if the weather is fine, take an early-evening stroll along Radical Rd at the foot of Salisbury Crags, or head up the stairs from nearby Calton Rd to the summit of Calton Hill (p76). Both offer superb views across the city.

Round off the day with dinner at a restaurant with a view, such as Tower (p44). If the weather's not so hot try somewhere more cosy and romantic, like Witchery by the Castle (p43) or Ondine (p42). Either pre- or post-dinner, scare yourself silly on a ghost tour of Greyfriars Kirkyard (p41), then head to the Bongo Club (p46) or Cabaret Voltaire (p45) for some alternative-style entertainment.

Day Two

Make morning number two a feast of culture. Tour the revamped exhibits in the National Museum of Scotland (p30), followed by a stroll down the Mound, with great views across Princes Street Gardens and the New Town to the iconic artworks of the Scottish National Gallery (p74).

Try a lunch of haggis or Cullen skink in the gallery's Scottish Cafe & Restaurant (p69), then work off those calories by climbing the nearby Scott Monument (p69) for stunning panoramic views. Catch a bus on Princes St and head to Ocean Terminal for a visit to the Royal Yacht Britannia (p106). Time your trip to get the last two hours of opening at *Britannia*, then head for a prebooked dinner.

Choose from one of Leith's many fine restaurants – Martin Wishart (p109) for fine French dining or Fishers Bistro (p109) for fresh seafood. Stay in Leith for a pint at Teuchters Landing (p111) or a cocktail in a teapot at the Roseleaf (p110), or head back to the city centre to sample some Edinburgh-brewed beer in the magnificent surroundings of the Café Royal Circle Bar (p80).

Short on time?

We've arranged Edinburgh's must-sees into these day-by-day itineraries to make sure you see the very best of the city in the time you have available.

Day Three

☀ Fingers crossed for good weather – begin the day with a visit to the **Scottish National Gallery of Modern Art** (p80), then enjoy a surprisingly bucolic walk along the Water of Leith Walkway to Stockbridge. Here you can explore the boutiques on St Stephen St before pausing for lunch at **Scran & Scallie** (p101), or enjoy a pub lunch in the **Stockbridge Tap** (p102).

☀ If it's Sunday spend an hour or so browsing the stalls at **Stockbridge Market** (p99), then make the short stroll to the **Royal Botanic Garden** (p96). If you didn't have lunch in Stockbridge, head to the garden's **Gateway Restaurant** or **Terrace Cafe**. This is one of the UK's leading botanic gardens, so devote the rest of the afternoon to exploring the palm houses, rock gardens, woodland gardens and outdoor sculptures.

☾ In the evening treat yourself to a decadent dinner at Michelin-starred **Castle Terrace** (p90) or stylishly rustic **Timberyard.** (p90) Have tickets booked for a show at the **Royal Lyceum Theatre** (p92) or the **Traverse** (p92), or else head for late-night Scottish folk music and dancing at **Ghillie Dhu** (p91).

Day Four

☀ Head to the southern fringes of the city and devote an entire morning to *The Da Vinci Code* delights of **Rosslyn Chapel** (p122). This 15th-century church is a monument to the stonemason's art, and so crammed with arcane symbolism that it has inspired countless conspiracy theories about possible links to the Knights Templar and the quest for the Holy Grail. Have lunch at the chapel's **coffee shop** (p123).

☀ Return to the city centre to spend the afternoon browsing the boutiques and department stores of the New Town, while soaking up the atmosphere of the world's best-preserved Georgian townscape. Take an hour or so to wander around the **Scottish National Portrait Gallery** (p66), which takes you on an entertaining journey through Scottish history via portraits of famous personalities.

☾ Take an early-evening stroll through **Princes Street Gardens** (p68) then wander down Leith Walk to **Joseph Pearce's** (p81) for a gin and tonic before tucking into a tasty organic dinner at **Gardener's Cottage** (p77) (book ahead). Round off the evening with some live jazz at **Jam House** (p82) or a comedy act at the **Stand** (p82).

Need to Know

For more information, see Survival Guide (p145)

Currency
Pound sterling (£). 100 pence = £1

Language
English

Visas
Generally not needed for stays of up to six months. Not a member of the Schengen Zone.

Money
ATMs widespread. Major credit cards accepted everywhere.

Mobile Phones
Uses the GSM 900/1800 network. Local SIM cards can be used in European and Australian phones.

Time
Edinburgh is on GMT; during British Summer Time (BST; last Sunday in March to last Saturday in October) clocks are one hour ahead of GMT.

Tipping
Tip restaurant waiting staff 10% to 15% unless service is included. Locals generally don't tip taxi drivers.

❶ Before You Go

Your Daily Budget

Budget less than £50
► Dorm beds £15–30
► Markets, lunch specials for food
► Loads of free museums and galleries

Midrange £50–150
► Double room £80–100
► Two-course dinner with glass of wine £30
► Live music in pub free–£10

Top End more than £150
► Double room in boutique/four-star hotel £175–225
► Three-course dinner in top restaurant including wine £70–100
► Taxi across town £15

Useful Websites

Lonely Planet (www.lonelyplanet.com/edinburgh) Destination info, hotel bookings, great for planning.

This Is Edinburgh (www.edinburgh.org) Official guide to the city.

The List (www.list.co.uk) Listings and reviews for restaurants, bars, clubs and theatres.

Advance Planning

Six months Book accommodation for August festival period. Book a table at the Witchery by the Castle.

Two months Book accommodation, reserve tables in top restaurants, book car hire.

One month Buy tickets online for Edinburgh Castle and Rosslyn Chapel, check listings for entertainment and book tickets.

② Arriving in Edinburgh

Most visitors arrive at Edinburgh Airport (www.edinburghairport.com), 8 miles west of the city centre, or at Edinburgh Waverley train station, right in the heart of the city between the Old Town and New Town.

✈ At the Airport

The arrivals hall has a tourist information and accommodation desk, left-luggage facilities, ATMs, currency exchange desks, shops, restaurants, internet access and car-hire agencies. Turn left out of arrivals to find the Airlink Bus 100 stop and the taxi ranks.

✈ From Edinburgh Airport

Destination	Best Transport
Old Town	Airlink Bus 100 or tram
New Town	Airlink Bus 100 or tram
West End	Airlink Bus 100, or tram
South Edinburgh	Airlink Bus 100 or tram, then connecting bus or taxi
Leith	Airlink Bus 100 or tram, then connecting bus or taxi

🚌 From Edinburgh Waverley Train Station

Taxi rank in station. Short walk to Princes St, where trams and buses depart to all areas of the city.

③ Getting Around

Edinburgh's public transport system consists of an extensive bus network and a single tram line. Lothian Buses (www.lothianbuses.com) runs most of the city bus routes, while First Edinburgh (www.firstedinburgh.co.uk) buses mainly serve towns and villages around Edinburgh. The tram line is operated by Edinburgh Trams (www.edinburghtrams.com).

🚌 Bus

The bus network is extensive, and is the best way of getting from the suburbs to the centre, and for north–south trips. Despite dedicated bus lanes, buses can get held up in traffic during rush hours.

🚋 Tram

Fast and frequent (every 10 to 12 minutes) service from the airport to York Place in the east of the city centre, via Murrayfield Stadium, Haymarket, the West End and Princes St.

🚗 Taxi

Friendly and knowledgeable drivers, great for late-night journeys, but fares can be expensive unless there are four people sharing.

🚲 Bicycle

Great for leisure – hire a bike and escape to the countryside via the Water of Leith Walkway, or the Union Canal towpath.

🚗 Car & Motorcycle

As a visitor, it's unlikely you'll need to drive. Disincentives include the difficulty of finding a parking place, high parking charges, and traffic congestion, especially during rush hours.

Edinburgh Neighbourhoods

New Town (p64)

Georgian terraces lined with designer boutiques, wine bars and cocktail lounges, plus Princes Street Gardens and the perfect viewpoint of Calton Hill.

⊙ **Top Sights**

Scottish National Portrait Gallery

Princes Street Gardens

Stockbridge (p94)

A former village with its own distinct identity, stylish and quirky shops and a good choice of pubs and restaurants.

⊙ **Top Sights**

Royal Botanic Garden

West End & Dean Village (p84)

More Georgian elegance and upmarket shops, leading down to the picturesque Dean Village in the wooded valley of the Water of Leith.

⊙ **Top Sights**

Scottish National Gallery of Modern Art

South Edinburgh (p112)

A peaceful residential area of Victorian tenement flats and spacious garden villas; not much in the way of tourist attractions, but good walking territory and many good restaurants and pubs.

⊙ Royal Botanic Garden

Scottish National Gallery of Modern Art

Princes Street Gardens

⊙ Edinburgh Castle

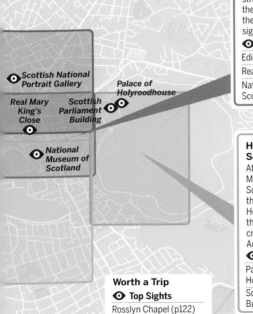

Royal Yacht Britannia

Leith (p104)
Redeveloped industrial docklands now occupied by restaurants, bars and Ocean Terminal, the city's biggest shopping centre.

⊙ Top Sights

Royal Yacht Britannia

Old Town (p22)
A maze of narrow wynds (alleys) and cobbled streets, strung out along the Royal Mile, home to the city's main historical sights.

⊙ Top Sights

Edinburgh Castle

Real Mary King's Close

National Museum of Scotland

Scottish National Portrait Gallery

Real Mary King's Close

Scottish Parliament Building

Palace of Holyroodhouse

National Museum of Scotland

Holyrood & Arthur's Seat (p52)
At the foot of the Royal Mile, contains the Scottish Parliament and the Palace of Holyroodhouse, and is the gateway to the craggy parkland of Arthur's Seat.

⊙ Top Sights

Palace of Holyroodhouse

Scottish Parliament Building

Worth a Trip
⊙ Top Sights

Rosslyn Chapel (p122)

Explore
Edinburgh

Worth a Trip

Edinburgh's oldest street, the Royal Mile (p39)
MATTHI/SHUTTERSTOCK ©

Explore

Old Town

Edinburgh's Old Town is a jagged, jumbled maze of historic masonry riddled with closes, stairs, vaults and wynds (narrow alleys) leading off the cobbled ravine of the Royal Mile, which links Edinburgh Castle to the Palace of Holyroodhouse. The restored 16th- and 17th-century Old Town tenements support a thriving city-centre community, crammed at street level with museums, restaurants, bars and shops.

The Sights in a Day

☀ Be at **Edinburgh Castle** (p24) for opening time and plan on spending two hours exploring its many attractions before heading downhill along the Royal Mile, stopping off as the fancy takes you at the **Scotch Whisky Experience** (p38), **Camera Obscura** (p42) and **Gladstone's Land** (p38).

☼ Continue down the Royal Mile, taking a quick look at **St Giles Cathedral** (p38) and **John Knox House** (p40) before taking a tour of either **Real Mary King's Close** (p28) or the **National Museum of Scotland** (p30). Get your photo taken beside the statue of **Greyfriars Bobby** (p41) and then take a stroll around **Greyfriars Kirkyard** (p41), before heading down to the Grassmarket for a drink and a look at the shops in atmospheric Victoria St.

☾ Book a late dinner at either **Ondine** (p42), **Witchery by the Castle** (p43) or **Wedgwood** (p43), and join a ghost tour of **Greyfriars Kirkyard** (p41) to work up an appetite. Or dine around 7pm then head to **Sandy Bell's** (p46) for some live Scottish folk music.

For a local's day in the Old Town, see p34

👁 Top Sights

Edinburgh Castle (p24)

Real Mary King's Close (p28)

National Museum of Scotland (p30)

⬤ Local Life

Explore the Old Town's Hidden History (p34)

♥ Best of Edinburgh

Eating

Ondine (p42)

Cannonball Restaurant (p43)

Grain Store (p44)

Mums (p43)

Wedgwood (p43)

Museums & Galleries

National Museum of Scotland (p30)

Museum of Edinburgh (p38)

Getting There

🚌 **Bus** Lothian bus 35 runs along the lower part of the Royal Mile from George IV Bridge to the Palace of Holyroodhouse; bus 6 links Hanover St in the New Town to the Scottish Parliament via Market St, St Mary's St and Holyrood Rd. Buses 23, 27, 41 and 42 run along the Mound and George IV Bridge, giving access to the Royal Mile and Grassmarket (via Victoria St or Candlemaker Row).

Top Sights
Edinburgh Castle

The brooding black crags of Castle Rock, rising above the western end of Princes St, are the very reason for Edinburgh's existence. This rocky hill was the most easily defended hilltop on the invasion route between England and central Scotland. Today it is one of Scotland's most atmospheric and popular tourist attractions.

👁 Map p36, A3

www.edinburghcastle.gov.uk

adult/child £16.50/9.90, audioguide additional £3.50

🕘9.30am-6pm Apr-Sep, to 5pm Oct-Mar, last admission 1hr before closing

🚌23, 27, 41, 42

The Esplanade

The castle's Esplanade is a parade ground dating from 1820, with superb views south over the city towards the Pentland Hills. At its western end is the **Entrance Gateway**, dating from 1888 and flanked by statues of Robert the Bruce and William Wallace. Above the gate is the Royal Standard of Scotland – a red lion rampant on a gold field – and the Scottish Royal motto in Latin, 'Nemo me impune lacessit'. This translates into Scots as 'wha daur meddle wi' me', and into English as 'watch it, pal' (OK, it literally means 'no one provokes me with impunity').

One O'Clock Gun

Inside the entrance a cobbled lane leads up beneath the 16th-century **Portcullis Gate**, topped by the 19th-century **Argyle Tower**, and past the cannon of the Argyle and Mills Mount Batteries. The battlements here have great views over the New Town to the Firth of Forth. At the far end of Mills Mount Battery is the OneO'Clock Gun, a gleaming WWII 25-pounder that fires an ear-splitting time signal at 1pm every day (except Sundays, Christmas Day and Good Friday).

St Margaret's Chapel

South of Mills Mount, the road curls up leftwards through **Foog's Gate** to the highest part of Castle Rock, crowned by the tiny **St Margaret's Chapel**, the oldest surviving building in Edinburgh. It's a simple Romanesque structure that is thought to have been built by David I or Alexander I in memory of their mother, Queen Margaret, sometime around 1130 (she was canonised in 1250). Following Cromwell's capture of the castle in 1650, the chapel was used to store ammunition until it was re-dedicated at the order of Queen Victoria; it was re-dedicated in 1934. The tiny stained-glass windows – depicting Queen Margaret, St Andrew,

☑ **Top Tips**

▶ Avoid ticket-office queues by purchasing your tickets online via the Edinburgh Castle website.

▶ It's worth hiring an audioguide to provide extra context for the various historical attractions you will see.

▶ Time your visit to coincide with the firing of the One O'Clock Gun.

✕ **Take a Break**

The **Tea Rooms at Edinburgh Castle** (Crown Sq; mains £9-15; ☉10am-5pm; ♦) serves good lunches.

Just a few yards downhill from the castle on the Royal Mile, Cannonball Restaurant (p43) offers top-quality Scottish cuisine.

Understand
Stone of Destiny

On St Andrew's Day 1996, with much pomp and ceremony, a block of sandstone 26.5 inches by 16.5 inches by 11 inches in size (67cm by 42cm by 28cm), with rusted iron hoops at either end, was installed in Edinburgh Castle. For the previous 700 years it had lain beneath the Coronation Chair in London's Westminster Abbey, where almost every English – and later British – monarch from Edward II in 1308 to Elizabeth II in 1953, had sat during their coronation ceremonies.

This is the legendary Stone of Destiny, on which Scottish kings placed their feet during their coronation (not their bums; the English got that bit wrong). It was stolen from Scone Abbey near Perth by King Edward I of England in 1296 and taken to London, where it remained for seven centuries, an enduring symbol of Scotland's subjugation by England.

It returned to the political limelight in 1996, when the Westminster government arranged for its return in an attempt to boost the flagging popularity of the Conservative Party in Scotland prior to a general election. (The stunt failed – Scotland returned no Conservative MPs at the ensuing election.)

St Columba, St Ninian and William Wallace – date from the 1920s.

Mons Meg

Immediately north of St Margaret's Chapel is Mons Meg, a giant 15th-century siege gun built at Mons in Belgium in 1449. The gun was last fired in 1681 as a birthday salute for the future King James VII/II, when its barrel burst. Take a peek over the wall to the north of the chapel and you'll see a charming little garden that was used as a **pet cemetery** for officers' dogs.

Great Hall

The main group of buildings on the summit of Castle Rock is ranged around Crown Sq, dominated by the shrine of the **Scottish National War Memorial**. Opposite is the Great Hall, built for James IV (r 1488–1513) as a ceremonial hall and used as a meeting place for the Scottish parliament until 1639. Its most remarkable feature is the original 16th-century hammer-beam roof.

Prisons of War Exhibition

The **Castle Vaults** beneath the Great Hall (entered on the west side of Crown Sq) were used variously as storerooms, bakeries and prisons. The vaults have been restored to how they were in the 18th and early-19th centuries, when they were used as a prison for soldiers captured during the American War of Independence and the Napoleonic Wars. Original graffiti, carved by French and American prisoners, can be seen on the ancient wooden doors.

Edinburgh Castle

Map labels:
- One O'Clock Gun
- Castle Bank
- West Princes Street Gardens
- Argyle Battery
- Cart Shed & Cafe
- Portcullis Gate & Argyle Tower
- Pet Cemetery
- Castle Gift Shop
- National War Museum
- Mons Meg
- St Margaret's Chapel
- Ticket Office
- Governor's House
- Castle Esplanade
- New Barracks
- Foog's Gate
- Scottish National War Memorial
- Entrance Gateway
- Royal Scots Museum
- Crown Square
- Half Moon Battery
- Military Prison
- Royal Palace
- Prisons of War Exhibition
- Great Hall
- King's Stables Rd
- Johnston Tce

Honours of Scotland

The **Royal Palace**, built during the 15th and 16th centuries, houses a series of historical tableaux leading to the highlight of the castle – a strongroom housing the Honours of Scotland (the Scottish Crown Jewels), the oldest surviving Crown Jewels in Europe. Locked away in a chest following the *Act of Union* in 1707, the crown (made in 1540 from the gold of Robert the Bruce's 14th-century coronet), sword and sceptre lay forgotten until they were unearthed at the instigation of the novelist Sir Walter Scott in 1818. Also on display here is the **Stone of Destiny**.

Among the neighbouring **Royal Apartments** is the bedchamber where Mary, Queen of Scots gave birth to her son James VI, who was to unite the crowns of Scotland and England in 1603.

Top Sights
Real Mary King's Close

Edinburgh's 18th-century city chambers were built over the sealed-off remains of Mary King's Close, and the lower levels of this medieval Old Town alley have survived almost unchanged amid the foundations for 250 years. Now open to the public, this spooky, subterranean labyrinth gives a fascinating insight into the everyday life of 17th-century Edinburgh.

👁 Map p36, D3

📞 0845 070 6244

www.realmarykingsclose.com

2 Warriston's Close, High St

adult/child £14.50/8.75

🕙 10am-9pm daily Apr-Oct, 10am-5pm Sun-Thu, 10am-9pm Fri & Sat Nov-Mar

🚌 23, 27, 41, 42

The Tenement Room

A costumed drama student in period costume will take you on a guided tour through the vaults, while practising his or her dramatic enunciation. The scripted tour, complete with ghostly tales and gruesome tableaux, can seem a little naff, milking the scary and scatological aspects of the close's history for all they're worth. But there are many things of genuine interest to see; there's something about the crumbling 17th-century tenement room that makes the hairs rise on the back of your neck, with tufts of horsehair poking from the collapsing lath-and-plaster walls, which bear the ghost of a pattern, and the ancient smell of stone and dust thick in your nostrils.

Wee Annie's Room

In one of the former bedrooms off the close, a psychic once claimed to have been approached by the ghost of a little girl called Annie. It's hard to tell what's more frightening – the story of the ghostly child, or the bizarre heap of tiny dolls and teddies left in a corner by sympathetic visitors.

The Foot of the Close

Perhaps the most atmospheric part of the tour is at the end, when you stand at the foot of Mary King's Close itself. You are effectively standing in a buried street with the old tenement walls rising on either side, and the weight of the 11 storeys of the city chambers above – and some 250 years of history – pressing down all around you.

☑ Top Tips

▶ Tours are limited to 20 people at a time, so book online at least 48 hours in advance to secure a place; to book within 48 hours, phone.

▶ The tour includes a lot of stairs and uneven stone surfaces – wear suitable shoes.

▶ There are lots of enclosed spaces – not recommended if you suffer from claustrophobia!

▶ Children under the age of five are not admitted.

✕ Take a Break

Enjoy pizza at a pavement table at **Gordon's Trattoria** (☏ 0131-225 7992; www.gordonstrattoria.com; 231 High St; mains £9-22; ⊘ noon-11pm Sun-Thu, to midnight Fri & Sat; 👪; 🚌 all South Bridge buses), a short distance downhill.

For a more sophisticated seafood lunch, head to Ondine (p42), uphill and round the corner.

Top Sights
National Museum of Scotland

The golden stone and striking modern architecture of the National Museum's new building (opened in 1998) make it one of the city's most distinctive landmarks. The museum's five floors trace the history of Scotland from geological beginnings to the 1990s. The new building connects with the recently renovated original Victorian museum, which covers natural history, world cultures, archaeology, and scientific and industrial technology.

◉ Map p37, E4

www.nms.ac.uk

Chambers St

fee for special exhibitions varies

🕘10am-5pm; 🚻

🚌2, 23, 27, 35, 41, 42, 45

Grand Gallery

The museum's main entrance, in the middle of Chambers St, leads into an atmospheric entrance hall occupying what used to be the museum cellars. Stairs lead up into the light of the Victorian Grand Gallery, a spectacular glass-roofed atrium lined with cast-iron pillars and balconies; this was the centrepiece of the original Victorian museum. It was designed in the 1860s by Captain Francis Fowke of the Royal Engineers, who also created the Royal Albert Hall in London, and parts of London's Victoria and Albert Museum.

Crowds gather on the hour to watch the chiming of the **Millennium Clock Tower**. Built in 1999 to commemorate the best and worst of human history, and inspired by mechanical marvels such as Prague's Astronomical Clock, it is more of a kinetic sculpture than a clock, crammed with amusing and thought-provoking symbols and animated figures.

Animal World

A door at the east end of the Grand Gallery leads into Animal World, one of the most impressive of the Victorian museum's new exhibits. No dusty, static regiments of stuffed creatures here, but a beautiful and dynamic display of animals apparently caught in the act of bounding, leaping or pouncing, arranged in groups that illustrate different means of locomotion, methods of feeding and modes of reproduction. Extinct creatures, including a full-size skeleton of a Tyrannosaurus rex, mingle with the living.

Window on the World

The exhibits ranged around the balconies of the Grand Gallery are billed as a 'Window on the World', showcasing more than 800 items from

☑ Top Tips

▶ Begin at the main entrance in the middle of Chambers St, rather than the modern tower at the west end of the street. You'll find an info desk with maps and leaflets, a cloakroom, toilets and a cafe-restaurant.

▶ Free, one-hour guided tours of the museum depart at 11am, 1pm and 3pm, each covering a different theme; ask for details at the info desk.

▶ You can download PDFs of museum trails for children to follow, and a National Museum of Scotland Highlights app for iOS and Android.

✗ Take a Break

The **Museum Brasserie** (☎0131-225 4040; www. benugo.com/restaurants/ museum-brasserie; mains £7-11; 🚼) in the basement of the Victorian part of the museum serves light lunches.

Tower (p44), in the modern half, is more formal and has an outdoor terrace with stunning views over the city.

the museum's collections, from the **world's largest scrimshaw carving**, occupying two full-size sperm whale jawbones, to a four-seat racing bicycle dating from 1898.

Hawthornden Court

A brand new suite of science and technology galleries link the Grand Gallery of the old museum to Hawthornden Court in the new building, with exhibits that include Dolly the Sheep, the first mammal ever to be cloned, and a section of a particle accelerator from CERN (the European Organization for Nuclear Research).

Early People Gallery

Stairs at the far end of Hawthornden Court lead down to the Early People Gallery on Level 0, decorated with intriguing humanoid sculptures by Sir Eduardo Paolozzi and beautiful installations by sculptor Andy Goldsworthy, including huge stacks of old roofing slates, cleverly arranged scrap timber and a sphere made entirely of whale bones.

Look for the **Cramond Lioness**, a Roman funerary sculpture of a lion gripping a human head in her jaws (it was discovered in the River Almond, on the western edge of Edinburgh, in 1997), and the 22kg of Roman silver that makes up the **Traprain Treasure**: it was buried in the 5th century AD and discovered in 1919, and is the biggest known hoard of Roman silver ever to be found.

Kingdom of the Scots

From the Early People Gallery, you work your way upwards through the history of Scotland. Highlights of the medieval Kingdom of the Scots galleries, on Levels 1 and 2, include the **Monymusk Reliquary**, a tiny silver casket dating from AD 750, which is said to have been carried into battle with Robert the Bruce at Bannockburn in 1314; and the famous **Lewis Chessmen**, a set of charming 12th-century chess pieces carved from walrus ivory that was discovered on Uig beach on the Isle of Lewis.

Daith Comes In...

The Daith Comes In (Death Comes In) exhibit on Level 4 is a goth's paradise of wooden hearses, jet jewellery and mourning bracelets made from human hair, as well as the 'mortsafes' that once protected newly buried corpses from the ravages of body-snatchers.

But the most fascinating objects on display here are the mysterious **Arthur's Seat coffins**. Discovered in a cave in 1836 by some boys hunting rabbits, these miniature coffins (only eight of the original 17 survive) are less than 10cm long and complete with tiny wooden figures inside. They may have been a mock burial for the victims of Edinburgh's most famous body-snatchers, Burke and Hare, who sold their murdered victims to the city's anatomy professor.

Leaving Scotland

Level 6 of the museum is given over to the 20th century, with galleries devoted to war, industry and daily life illustrated by personal stories, film clips and iconic objects such as a **set of bagpipes** that was played at the Battle of the Somme in 1916. There is also an exhibition called Leaving Scotland, containing stories of the Scottish diaspora who emigrated to begin new lives in Canada, Australia, the USA and other places, from the 18th century right up until the 1960s.

Roof Terrace

Before you leave, find the elevator in the corner of Level 6, near the war gallery, and go up to the roof terrace to enjoy a fantastic view across the city to the castle ramparts.

Local Life
Explore the Old Town's Hidden History

Edinburgh's Old Town extends to the south of the Royal Mile, descending into the valley of the Grassmarket and Cowgate, which is crossed by the arches of George IV Bridge and South Bridge. This difference in levels has created a maze of narrow closes, wynds and staircases, which lend an adventurous air to exploring its many hidden corners.

❶ Victoria Terrace

From the Lawnmarket at the top of the Royal Mile, dive down Fisher's Close, which leads you onto the delightful Victoria Terrace, strung above the cobbled curve of shop-lined Victoria St. Wander along to the right, enjoying the view – **Maxie's Bistro** (📞0131-226 7770; www.maxiesbistro.com; 5b Johnston Tce; mains £9-22; ⏰11am-11pm; 🛜♿; 🚌23, 27, 41, 42), at the far end of the terrace, is a great place to stop for lunch or a drink.

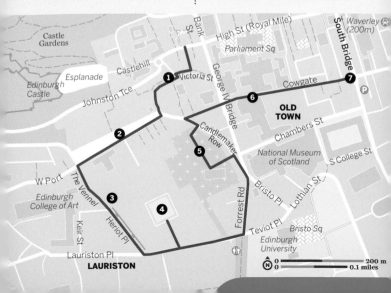

❷ Grassmarket

Descend the stairs in the middle of the terrace and continue downhill to the Grassmarket. The site of a cattle market from the 15th century until the start of the 20th, the Grassmarket was also the city's place of execution, and martyred Covenanters are commemorated by a monument at the eastern end, where the gallows once stood. The notorious murderers Burke and Hare operated from a now-vanished close off the west end.

❸ Flodden Wall

Turn left up the flight of stairs known as the Vennel. At the top of the steps on the left you'll find the Flodden Wall, one of the few surviving fragments of the city wall that was built in the early 16th century as protection against a feared English invasion. Beyond it stretches the Telfer Wall, a later extension.

❹ George Heriot's School

Turn left along Lauriston Pl to find George Heriot's School, one of the most impressive buildings in the Old Town. Built in the 17th century with funds bequeathed by George Heriot (goldsmith and banker to King James VI, and popularly known as Jinglin' Geordie), it was originally a school for orphaned children, but became a fee-paying school in 1886. It is open to the public on Doors Open Day (www.doorsopendays.org.uk) in September.

❺ Greyfriars Kirkyard

Hemmed in by high walls and overlooked by the castle, Greyfriars Kirkyard is one of Edinburgh's most evocative spots, a peaceful green oasis dotted with elaborate monuments. Many famous Edinburgh names are buried here, including poet Allan Ramsay (1686–1758) and William Smellie (1740–95), editor of the first edition of Encyclopaedia Britannica.

❻ Cowgate

The Cowgate – the long, dark ravine leading eastwards from the Grassmarket – was once the road along which cattle were driven from the pastures around Arthur's Seat to the safety of the city walls, or to be sold at market. To the right are the new law courts, followed by Tailors Hall (built 1621, extended 1757), now a hotel and bar but formerly the meeting place of the 'Companie of Tailzeours' (Tailors' Guild).

❼ South Bridge Vaults

South Bridge passes over the Cowgate in a single arch, but there are another nine arches hidden on either side, surrounded by later buildings. The ones to the north can be visited on a guided tour with **Mercat Tours** (p144); those to the south are occupied by a nightclub, **Caves** (Map p36, F3; ☏ 0131-557 8989; www.thecavesedinburgh.com; 8-12 Niddry St South; 🚌 35).

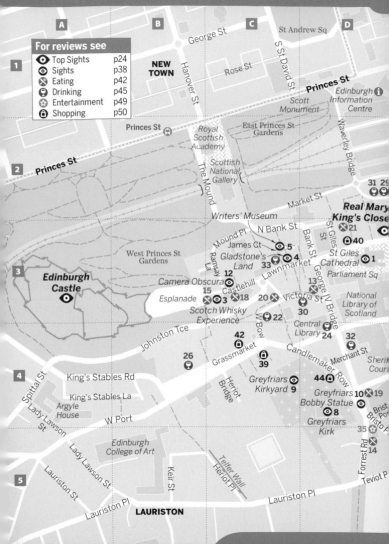

A **B** **C** **D**

George St

St Andrew Sq

NEW TOWN

Rose St

Hanover St

S St David St

Princes St

For reviews see

1

Edinburgh Information Centre

Scott Monument

Princes St

Royal Scottish Academy

East Princes St Gardens

Waverley Bridge

2 Princes St

The Mound

Scottish National Gallery

Market St

31 29

Real Mary King's Close

Writers' Museum

Mound Pl

N Bank St

21

West Princes St Gardens

Ramsay La

James Ct

Gladstone's Land

5

40

4

33

Lawnmarket

St Giles Cathedral

Bank St

St Giles St

George IV Bridge

1

Parliament Sq

3 **Edinburgh Castle**

15

Camera Obscura

12

Castlehill

13

Esplanade

3

18

20

Victoria St

National Library of Scotland

Scotch Whisky Experience

22

30

W Bow

Central Library

24

32

Johnston Tce

42

Candlemaker Row

Merchant St

4 King's Stables Rd

26

Grassmarket

39

Heriot Bridge

44

Sheriff Court

Greyfriars Kirkyard

9

Greyfriars 10 19
Bobby Statue

8

Greyfriars Kirk

35

Spittal St

Lady Lawson St

King's Stables La

Argyle House

W Port

Bristo Pow

Bristo P

Forrest Rd

14

Edinburgh College of Art

Heriot Pl

Telfer Wall

Keir St

5

Lauriston St

Lauriston Pl

Teviot P

Lauriston Pl

LAURISTON

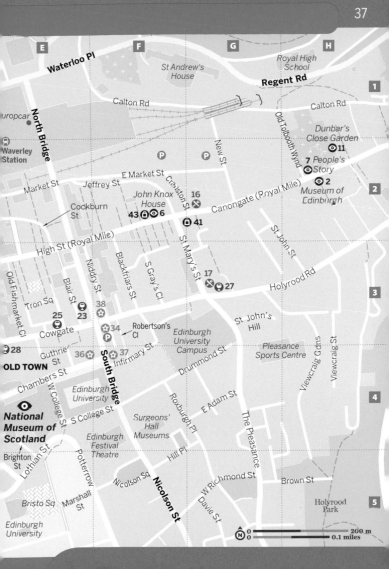

E Waterloo Pl
St Andrew's House
F
G
Royal High School
Regent Rd
H

Calton Rd
1
Calton Rd

uropcar
North Bridge
Old Tolbooth Wynd
Dunbar's Close Garden
◉11

Waverley Station
P
New St
7 People's Story

E Market St
Cranston St
◉2
Museum of Edinburgh

Market St
Jeffrey St
John Knox House
16
Canongate (Royal Mile)
St John St
2

Cockburn St
43 ⦿ ◉ 6
St Mary's St
🔒41

High St (Royal Mile)
Holyrood Rd
3

Old Fishmarket Cl
Blair St
Niddry St
Blackfriars St
S Gray's Cl
17
🍴27

Tron Sq
38
23
St John's Hill
Holyrood Rd

25
34
Robertson's Cl
Edinburgh University Campus
Pleasance Sports Centre
Viewcraig Gdns
Viewcraig St

Cowgate
P
4

28
Guthrie St
36 ⭐ 37
South Bridge
Infirmary St
Drummond St
St
E Adam St
The Pleasance

OLD TOWN
Chambers St
W College St
Edinburgh University
Roxburgh Pl

National Museum of Scotland
S College St
Surgeons' Hall Museums
Hill Pl
Brown St

Brighton St
Lothian St
Edinburgh Festival Theatre
W Richmond St
Holyrood Park

Bristo Sq
Potterrow
Nicolson Sq
Marshall St
Nicolson St
Davie St
5

Edinburgh University
🧭 0   200 m
0   0.1 miles

Sights

St Giles Cathedral CHURCH

1 ◎ Map p36, D3

The great grey bulk of St Giles Cathedral dates largely from the 15th century, but much of it was restored in the 19th century. One of the most interesting corners of the kirk is the **Thistle Chapel**, built in 1911 for the Knights of the Most Ancient & Most Noble Order of the Thistle. The elaborately carved Gothic-style stalls have canopies topped with the helms and arms of the 16 knights – look out for the bagpipe-playing angel amid the vaulting. (www.stgilescathedral.org.uk; High St; suggested donation £3; ◷9am-7pm Mon-Fri, to 5pm Sat, 1-5pm Sun May-Sep, 9am-5pm Mon-Sat, 1-5pm Sun Oct-Apr; 🚍23, 27, 41, 42)

Museum of Edinburgh MUSEUM

2 ◎ Map p36, H2

You can't miss the colourful facade of Huntly House, brightly renovated in red and yellow ochre, opposite the Tolbooth clock on the Royal Mile. Built in 1570, it houses a museum covering Edinburgh from its prehistory to the present. Exhibits of national importance include an original copy of the National Covenant of 1638, but the big crowd-pleaser is the dog collar and feeding bowl that once belonged to Greyfriars Bobby (p41), the city's most famous canine citizen. (📞0131-529 4143; www.edinburghmuseums.org.uk; 142 Canongate; admission free; ◷10am-5pm Mon-Sat year-round, noon-5pm Sun Aug; 🚍35)

Scotch Whisky Experience MUSEUM

3 ◎ Map p36, C3

A former school houses this multimedia centre explaining the making of whisky from barley to bottle in a series of exhibits, demonstrations and talks that combine sight, sound and smell, including the world's largest collection of malt whiskies (3384 bottles!). More expensive tours include more extensive whisky tastings and samples of Scottish cuisine. There's also a restaurant (p44) that serves traditional Scottish dishes with, where possible, a dash of whisky thrown in. (www.scotchwhiskyexperience.co.uk; 354 Castlehill; adult/child incl tour & tasting £14.50/7.25; ◷10am-6pm Apr-Aug, to 5pm Sep-Mar; 📶; 🚍23, 27, 41, 42)

Gladstone's Land HISTORIC BUILDING

4 ◎ Map p36, C3

One of Edinburgh's most prominent 17th-century merchants was Thomas Gledstanes, who in 1617 purchased the tenement later known as Gladstone's Land. It contains fine painted ceilings, walls and beams, and some splendid furniture from the 17th and 18th centuries. The volunteer guides provide a wealth of anecdotes and a detailed history. (NTS; www.nts.org.uk/Property/Gladstones-Land; 477 Lawnmarket; adult/child £6.50/5; ◷10am-6.30pm Jul & Aug, to 5pm Apr-Jun & Sep-Oct; 🚍23, 27, 41, 42)

Understand

Old Town History

Before the founding of the New Town in the 18th century, old Edinburgh was an overcrowded and unsanitary hive of humanity. Constrained between the boggy ground of the Nor' Loch (now drained and occupied by Princes Street Gardens) to the north and the city walls to the south and east, the only way for the town to expand was upwards.

Old Town Tenements
The five- to eight-storey tenements that were raised along the Royal Mile in the 16th and 17th centuries were the skyscrapers of their day, remarked upon with wonder by visiting writers such as Daniel Defoe. All classes of society, from beggars to magistrates, lived cheek by jowl in these urban ants' nests, the wealthy occupying the middle floors – high enough to be above the noise and stink of the streets, but not so high that climbing the stairs would be too tiring – while the poor squeezed into attics, basements, cellars and vaults.

Royal Mile
The Royal Mile, Edinburgh's oldest street, connects the castle to the Palace of Holyroodhouse. It is split into four named sections: Castle-hill, the Lawnmarket, the High St and the Canongate.

A corruption of 'Landmarket', **Lawnmarket** takes its name from a large cloth market (selling goods from the land outside the city) that flourished here until the 18th century; this was the poshest part of the Old Town, where many distinguished citizens made their homes.

High Street, which stretches from George IV Bridge down to St Mary's St, is the heart and soul of the Old Town, home to the city's main church, the law courts, the city chambers and – until 1707 – the Scottish parliament. The Old Town's eastern gate, the Netherbow Port (part of the Flodden Wall), once stood at the Mary's St end. Though it no longer exists, its former outline is marked by brass strips set in the road.

Canongate – the section between the Netherbow and Holyrood – takes its name from the Augustinian canons (monks) of Holyrood Abbey. From the 16th century it was home to aristocrats who wanted to live near the Palace of Holyroodhouse.

Writers' Museum
MUSEUM

5 ◉ Map p36, C3

Tucked down a close between the Royal Mile and the Mound you'll find Lady Stair's House (1622), home to this museum that contains manuscripts and memorabilia belonging to three of Scotland's most famous writers: Robert Burns, Sir Walter Scott and Robert Louis Stevenson. (☎0131-529 4901; www.edinburghmuseums.org.uk; Lady Stair's Close, Lawnmarket; admission free; ◷10am-5pm Mon-Sat year-round, noon-5pm Sun Aug; ◻23, 27, 41, 42)

John Knox House
HISTORIC BUILDING

6 ◉ Map p36, F2

The Royal Mile narrows at the foot of High St beside the jutting facade of John Knox House. This is the oldest

---

☑ Top Tip

Ghost Tours

The City of the Dead (p144) tour of Greyfriars Kirkyard, run by Black Hart Storytellers, is probably the scariest of Edinburgh's ghost tours. Many people have reported encounters with the McKenzie Poltergeist, the ghost of a 17th-century judge who persecuted the Covenanters (supporters of the Scottish Presbyterian church, in defiance of King Charles I's attempts to impose Roman Catholicism) and now haunts their former prison in a corner of the kirkyard. Not suitable for young children!

---

surviving tenement in Edinburgh, dating from around 1490. John Knox, an influential church reformer and leader of the Protestant Reformation in Scotland, is thought to have lived here from 1561 to 1572. The labyrinthine interior has some beautiful painted-timber ceilings and an interesting display on Knox's life and work. (www.scottishstorytellingcentre.co.uk; 43-45 High St; adult/child £5/1; ◷10am-6pm Mon-Sat year-round, noon-6pm Sun Jul & Aug; ◻35)

People's Story
MUSEUM

7 ◉ Map p36, H2

One of the surviving symbols of the Canongate district's former independence is the **Canongate Tolbooth**. Built in 1591 it served successively as a collection point for tolls (taxes), a council house, a courtroom and a jail. With picturesque turrets and a projecting clock, it's an interesting example of 16th-century architecture. It now houses a fascinating museum called the People's Story, which covers the life, work and pastimes of ordinary Edinburgh folk from the 18th century to today. (www.edinburghmuseums.org.uk; 163 Canongate; admission free; ◷10am-5pm Mon-Sat year-round, noon-5pm Sun Aug; ◻35)

Greyfriars Kirk
CHURCH

8 ◉ Map p36, D4

One of Edinburgh's most famous churches, Greyfriars Kirk was built on the site of a Franciscan friary and opened for worship on Christmas

Day 1620. Surrounding the church, Greyfriars Kirkyard (p41) is one of Edinburgh's most evocative cemeteries. (www.greyfriarskirk.com; Candlemaker Row; admission free; ☉10.30am-4.30pm Mon-Fri, 11am-2pm Sat Apr-Oct, closed Nov-Mar; 🚌2, 23, 27, 35, 41, 42, 45)

Greyfriars Kirkyard CEMETERY

9 ◎ Map p36, C4

Greyfriars Kirkyard is one of Edinburgh's most evocative cemeteries, a peaceful green oasis dotted with elaborate monuments. Many famous Edinburgh names are buried here, including the poet Allan Ramsay (1686–1758), architect William Adam (1689–1748) and William Smellie (1740–95), the editor of the first edition of the *Encyclopedia Britannica*. If you want to experience the graveyard at its scariest – inside a burial vault, in the dark, at night – go on one of the City of the Dead (p144) guided tours. (www.greyfriarskirk.com; Candlemaker Row; ☉8am-dusk; 🚌2, 23, 27, 35, 41, 42, 45)

Greyfriars Bobby Statue MONUMENT

10 ◎ Map p36, D4

Probably the most popular photo opportunity in Edinburgh, the life-size statue of Greyfriars Bobby, a Skye terrier who captured the hearts of the British public in the late 19th century, stands outside Greyfriars Kirkyard (p41). From 1858 to 1872, the wee dog maintained a vigil over the grave of his master, an Edinburgh police officer.

☑ Top Tip

Parliament Hall

Before you visit the Scottish Parliament Building, take a look at the magnificent 17th-century **Parliament Hall** (☎0131-348 5355; 11 Parliament Sq; admission free; ☉10am-4pm Mon-Fri; 🚌2, 23, 27, 41, 42, 45). Tucked behind St Giles Cathedral, it has an original oak hammerbeam roof, and is where the original Scottish parliament met before its dissolution in 1707. Now used by lawyers and their clients as a meeting place, it's open to the public. As you enter (there's a sign outside saying 'Parliament Hall; Court of Session') you'll see the reception desk in front of you; the hall is through the double doors immediately on your right.

The story was immortalised in a novel by Eleanor Atkinson in 1912, and in 1963 was made into a movie by – who else? – Walt Disney. (cnr George IV Bridge & Candlemaker Row; 🚌2, 23, 27, 35, 41, 42, 45)

Dunbar's Close Garden GARDENS

11 ◎ Map p36, H2

Tucked away at the end of an Old Town close, this walled garden has been laid out in the style of the 17th century, with gravel paths, neatly trimmed shrubs, herbs, flowers and mature trees. A hidden gem, and an oasis of tranquillity amid the bustle of the Royal Mile. (Canongate; ☉24hr; 🚌35)

GIMAS/SHUTTERSTOCK©

View up the Royal Mile, with Camera Obscura to the left

Camera Obscura
MUSEUM

12 📍 Map p36, C3

Edinburgh's camera obscura (pictured above) is a curious 19th-century device – in constant use since 1853 – that uses lenses and mirrors to throw a live image of the city onto a large horizontal screen. The accompanying commentary is entertaining and the whole experience has a quirky charm, complemented by an intriguing exhibition dedicated to illusions of all kinds. Stairs lead up through various displays to the **Outlook Tower**, which offers great views over the city. (www.camera-obscura.co.uk; Castlehill; adult/child £14.50/10.50; ⊙9am-9pm Jul & Aug, 9.30am-7pm Apr-Jun & Sep-Oct, 10am-6pm Nov-Mar; 🚌23, 27, 41, 42)

Eating

Ondine
SEAFOOD ££££

13 🍴 Map p36, D3

Ondine is one of Edinburgh's finest seafood restaurants, with a menu based on sustainably sourced fish. Take a seat at the curved Oyster Bar and tuck into oysters Kilpatrick, smoked haddock chowder, lobster thermidor, a roast shellfish platter or just good old haddock and chips (with minted pea purée, just to keep things posh). (📞0131-226 1888; www.ondinerestaurant.co.uk; 2 George IV Bridge; mains £17-40, 2-/3-course lunch £25/30; 🕐noon-3pm & 5.30-10pm Mon-Sat; 🛜; 🚌23, 27, 41, 42)

Mums
CAFE £

14 🍴 Map p36, D5

This nostalgia-fuelled cafe serves up classic British comfort food that wouldn't look out of place on a 1950s menu – bacon and eggs, bangers and mash, shepherd's pie, fish and chips. But there's a twist – the food is all top-quality nosh freshly prepared from local produce. There's also a good selection of bottled craft beers and Scottish-brewed cider. (📞0131-260 9806; www.monstermashcafe.co.uk; 4a Forrest Rd; mains £8-11; 🕐9am-10pm Mon-Sat, 10am-10pm Sun; 🛜♿; 🚌23, 27, 41, 42)

Cannonball Restaurant
SCOTTISH ££

15 🍴 Map p36, C3

The historic Cannonball House next to Edinburgh Castle's esplanade has been transformed into a sophisticated restaurant (and whisky bar) where the Contini family work their Italian magic on Scottish classics to produce dishes such as haggis balls with spiced pickled turnip and whisky marmalade, and lobster with wild garlic and lemon butter. (📞0131-225 1550; www.contini.com/contini-cannonball; 356 Castlehill, Royal Mile; mains £15-25; 🕐noon-5pm & 5.30-10pm Tue-Sat; 🛜♿; 🚌23, 27, 41, 42)

Wedgwood
SCOTTISH £££

16 🍴 Map p36, G2

Fine food without the fuss is the motto at this friendly, unpretentious restaurant. Scottish produce is served with an inventive flair in dishes such as venison mince pie with black pudding mash and onion puree, or sesame and soy-glazed sea trout with crisped scallop roe, while the menu includes foraged wild salad leaves collected by the chef himself. (📞0131-558 8737; www.wedgwoodtherestaurant.co.uk; 267 Canongate; mains £17-23, 2-/3-course lunch £15/19; 🕐noon-3pm & 6-10pm; 🚌35)

David Bann
VEGETARIAN ££

17 🍴 Map p36, G3

If you want to convince a carnivorous friend that cuisine à la veg can be as tasty and inventive as a meat-muncher's menu, take them to David Bann's stylish restaurant – dishes such as Thai fritter of broccoli and smoked tofu, and aubergine, chickpea and cashew kofta are guaranteed to win converts. (📞0131-556 5888; www.davidbann.com; 56-58 St Mary's St; mains £11-13; 🕐noon-10pm Mon-Fri, 11am-10pm Sat & Sun; ♿; 🚌35)

Witchery by the Castle
SCOTTISH, FRENCH £££

18 🍴 Map p36, C3

Set in a merchant's town house dating from 1595, the Witchery is a candlelit corner of antique splendour with oak-panelled walls, low ceilings, opulent wall hangings and red leather upholstery; stairs lead down to a second, even more romantic, dining room called the Secret Garden. The menu ranges from oysters to Aberdeen Angus steak and the wine list runs to almost 1000 bins. (☏0131-225 5613; www.thewitchery.com; Castlehill; mains £23-45, 2-course lunch £20; ⊙noon-11.30pm; ☐23, 27, 41, 42)

Tower

SCOTTISH £££

19 🍴 Map p36, D4

Chic and sleek, with a great view of the castle, Tower is perched in a turret

---

Local Life
Edinburgh's Mysterious Book Sculptures

In 2011 and 2012 an unknown artist left a series of intricate and beautiful paper sculptures in various Edinburgh libraries, museums and bookshops (more sculptures appeared in 2013 and 2014). Each was fashioned from an old book and alluded to literary themes; a message from the anonymous artist revealed they had been inspired by the poem 'Gifts', by Edinburgh poet Norman MacCaig. Two are on display at the **Scottish Poetry Library** (www.spl. org.uk; 5 Crichton's Close, Canongate; admission free; ⊙10am-5pm Tue, Wed & Fri, to 7pm Thu, to 4pm Sat; ☏; ☐35, 36), where you can pick up a self-guided walking-tour leaflet, *Gifted: the Edinburgh Book Sculptures* (also available on its website).

---

atop the National Museum of Scotland building. A star-studded guest list of celebrities has enjoyed its menu of quality Scottish food, simply prepared – try half a dozen oysters followed by roast loin of venison. Afternoon tea (£20) is served from 2.30pm to 5.30pm. (☏0131-225 3003; www.tower-restaurant.com; National Museum of Scotland, Chambers St; mains £19-40, 2-course lunch & pre-theatre menu £19; ⊙10am-11pm; ☐2, 23, 27, 41, 42, 45)

Grain Store

SCOTTISH £££

20 🍴 Map p36, C3

An atmospheric upstairs dining room on picturesque Victoria St, the Grain Store has a well-earned reputation for serving the finest Scottish produce, perfectly prepared – from wood pigeon with leek and hickory risotto to seared monkfish with scallop ravioli and mustard beurre blanc. The three-course lunch for £16 is good value. (☏0131-225 7635; www.grainstore-restaurant.co.uk; 30 Victoria St; mains £20-32; ⊙noon-2.30pm & 6-9.45pm Mon-Sat, 6pm-9.30pm Sun; ☐2, 23, 27, 41, 42)

Amber

SCOTTISH ££

You've got to love a place (see 3 🍴 Map p36, C3) where the waiter greets you with the words, 'I'll be your whisky adviser for this evening'. Located in the Scotch Whisky Experience (p38), this whisky-themed restaurant manages to avoid the tourist clichés and creates genuinely interesting and flavoursome dishes using top Scottish produce, with a suggested whisky pairing for

Understand
The Resurrection Men

Edinburgh has long had a reputation for being at the cutting edge of medical research. In the early 19th century this led to a shortage of cadavers with which the city's anatomists could satisfy their curiosity, and an illegal trade in dead bodies emerged.

The readiest supply of corpses was to be found in the city's graveyards. Grave robbers – known as 'resurrection men' – plundered newly buried coffins and sold the cadavers to the anatomists, who turned a blind eye to the source of their research material.

William Burke and William Hare took the body-snatching business a step further, deciding to create their own supply of fresh cadavers by resorting to murder. Between December 1827 and October 1828 they killed at least 16 people, selling their bodies to the surgeon Robert Knox.

When the law finally caught up with them Hare testified against Burke, who was hanged outside St Giles Cathedral in January 1829. In an ironic twist, his body was given to the anatomy school for public dissection.

each dish. (📞0131-477 8477; www.amber-restaurant.co.uk; 354 Castlehill; mains £13-22; ⏰noon-8.30pm Sun-Thu, to 9pm Fri & Sat; 📶👪; 🚌23, 27, 41, 42)

Devil's Advocate
PUB FOOD ££

21 🍴 Map p36, D3

No trip to Edinburgh is complete without exploring the narrow closes (alleys) that lead off the Royal Mile. Lucky you if your explorations lead to this cosy split-level pub-restaurant set in a converted Victorian pump house, with a menu of top-quality pub grub – the burgers are among the best in town. It gets rammed on weekends, so book a table. (📞0131-225 4465; http://devilsadvocateedinburgh.co.uk; 9 Advocates Close; mains £14-24; ⏰food served noon-4pm & 5-10pm; 📶; 🚌6, 23, 27, 41, 42)

Drinking

Bow Bar
PUB

22 🍺 Map p36, C3

One of the city's best traditional-style pubs (it's not as old as it looks), serving a range of excellent real ales, Scottish craft gins and a vast selection of malt whiskies, the Bow Bar often has standing-room only on Friday and Saturday evenings. (www.thebowbar.co.uk; 80 West Bow; ⏰noon-midnight Mon-Sat, to 11.30pm Sun; 👪; 🚌2, 23, 27, 41, 42)

Cabaret Voltaire
CLUB

23 🍺 Map p36, E3

An atmospheric warren of stone lined vaults houses this self-consciously 'alternative' club, which eschews huge dance floors and egotistical DJ worship in favour of a 'creative crucible' hosting an eclectic mix of DJs, live acts, comedy, theatre, visual arts and the spoken word. Well worth a look. (www.thecabaretvoltaire.com; 36-38 Blair St; ☉5pm-3am Mon-Thu, noon-3am Fri-Sun; 🛜; 🚌all South Bridge buses)

Bongo Club CLUB

24 🚇 Map p36, D4

Owned by a local arts charity, the weird and wonderful Bongo Club boasts a long history of hosting everything from wild club nights and local bands to performance art and kids' comedy shows, and is open as a cafe and exhibition space during the day. (www.thebongoclub.co.uk; 66 Cowgate; admission free-£6; ☉11pm-3am Tue & Thu, 7pm-3am Fri-Sun; 🛜; 🚌2)

Local Life
Sandy Bell's

This unassuming **pub** (www.sandybellsedinburgh.co.uk; 25 Forrest Rd; ☉noon-1am Mon-Sat, 12.30pm-midnight Sun; 🚌2, 23, 27, 41, 42, 45) is a stalwart of the traditional music scene (the founder's wife sang with the Corries). There's music almost every evening at 9pm, and from 3pm Saturday and Sunday, plus lots of impromptu sessions.

OX 184 BAR

25 🚇 Map p36, E3

A big, booming industrial-chic bar with more than 100 whiskies on offer (Scotch, Irish, American and Japanese), as well as a fine selection of real ales and craft beers, the OX's standout feature is a huge wood-fired grill on which burgers, ribs and steaks are constantly sizzling. DJs and live bands every night . (📞0131-226 1645; www.ox184.co.uk; 184-186 Cowgate; ☉11am-3am; 🛜; 🚌35, 45)

White Hart Inn PUB

26 🚇 Map p36, B4

A brass plaque outside this pub proclaims: 'In the White Hart Inn Robert Burns stayed during his last visit to Edinburgh, 1791.' Claiming to be the city's oldest pub in continuous use (since 1516), it also hosted William Wordsworth in 1803. Not surprisingly, it's a traditional, cosy, low-raftered place. It has folk/acoustic music sessions seven nights a week. (📞0131-226 2806; www.whitehart-edinburgh.co.uk; 34 Grassmarket; ☉11am-11pm Mon-Fri, to 12.30am Sat & Sun; 🚌2)

Holyrood 9A PUB

27 🚇 Map p36, G3

Candlelight flickering off hectares of polished wood creates an atmospheric setting for this superb real-ale bar, with more than 20 taps pouring craft beers from all corners of the country and,

WILL ROBB/GETTY IMAGES ©

Brew Dog

indeed, the globe. If you're peckish, it serves excellent gourmet burgers too. (www.theholyrood.co.uk; 9a Holyrood Rd; ⏱9am-midnight Sun-Thu, to 1am Fri & Sat; 📶; 🚌36)

BrewDog
BAR

28 🚇 Map p36, E4

The Edinburgh outpost of Scotland's self-styled 'punk brewery', BrewDog (pictured above) stands out among the sticky-floored dives that line the Cowgate, with its polished concrete bar and cool, industrial-chic decor. As well as its own highly rated beers, there's a choice of guest real ales, and – a sign of a great trad pub – coat hooks under the edge of the bar. (www.brewdog.com; 143 Cowgate; ⏱noon-1am Mon-Sat, 12.30pm-1am Sun; 📶; 🚌35, 45)

Malt Shovel
PUB

29 🚇 Map p36, D2

A traditional-looking pub with dark wood and subdued tartanry, the Malt Shovel offers a good range of real ales and more than 40 malt whiskies, and serves excellent pub grub including fish and chips, burgers, and steak and ale pies. (📞0131-225 6843; www.taylor-walker.co.uk; 11-15 Cockburn St; ⏱11am-11pm Sun-Thu, to 1am Fri & Sat; 📶👪; 🚌36, 41)

Understand

Underground Edinburgh

As Edinburgh expanded in the late 18th and early 19th centuries, new bridges were built to link the Old Town to newly developed areas to its north and south. **South Bridge** (completed 1788) and **George IV Bridge** (1834) lead southwards from the Royal Mile over the deep valley of the Cowgate, but since their construction so many buildings have clustered around them that you can hardly tell they are bridges. George IV Bridge has a total of nine arches but only two are visible, and South Bridge has no less than 18 hidden arches.

These underground vaults were originally used as storerooms, workshops and drinking dens. But as early 19th-century Edinburgh's population swelled with an influx of penniless Highlanders cleared from their lands and Irish refugees from the potato famine, the dark, dripping chambers were given over to slum accommodation. The vaults were eventually cleared in the late 19th century, then lay forgotten until 1994 when some of the South Bridge vaults were opened to guided tours (from Mercat Tours (p35)), while others are now home to atmospheric nightclubs such as Cabaret Voltaire (p45) and Caves (p35).

Liquid Room

CLUB

30 🚇 Map p36, D3

Set in a subterranean vault deep beneath Victoria St, the Liquid Room is a superb club venue with a thundering sound system. There are regular club nights on Wednesday, Friday and Saturday, as well as live bands. (www.liquidroom.com; 9c Victoria St; admission free-£20; ☉live music from 7pm, club 10.30pm-3am Wed, Fri & Sat; 🚌23, 27, 41, 42)

Ecco Vino

WINE BAR

31 🚇 Map p36, D2

With outdoor tables on sunny afternoons and cosy candlelit intimacy in the evenings, this comfortably cramped Tuscan-style wine bar offers a tempting range of Italian wines, though not all are available by the glass. (www.eccovinoedinburgh.com; 19 Cockburn St; ☉noon-11pm Mon-Thu, to midnight Fri & Sat, 12.30-11pm Sun; 🛜; 🚌6)

Villager

BAR

32 🚇 Map p36, D4

A cross between a traditional pub and a pre-club bar, Villager has a comfortable, laid-back vibe. It can be standing-room only in the main bar in the evenings (the cocktails are excellent), but the side room, with its brown leather sofas and subtropical pot plants, comes into its own for a lazy Sunday afternoon with the papers. (www.villagerbar.com; 49-50 George IV Bridge; ☉noon-1am; 🛜; 🚌23, 27, 41, 42)

Jolly Judge
PUB

33 🚇 Map p36, C3

A snug little howff tucked away down a close, the Judge exudes a cosy 17th-century atmosphere (low, timber-beamed painted ceilings) and has the added attraction of a cheering open fire in cold weather No music or gaming machines, just the buzz of conver sation. (www.jollyjudge.co.uk; 7a James Ct; ⏰noon-11pm Mon-Thu, to midnight Fri & Sat, 12.30-11pm Sun; 📶; 🚌23, 27, 41, 42)

Entertainment

Caves
LIVE MUSIC

34 ⭐ Map p36, F3

A spectacular subterranean club venue set in the ancient stone vaults beneath the South Bridge, the Caves stages a series of one-off club nights and live-music gigs, as well as *ceilidh* nights during the festival – check the What's On link on the website for upcoming events. (☎0131-557 8989; www.thecavesedinburgh.com; 8-12 Niddry St South; 🚌35)

Bedlam Theatre
COMEDY

35 ⭐ Map p36, D5

The Bedlam hosts a long-established (more than 25 years) weekly improvisation slot, the Improverts, which is hugely popular with local students. Shows kick off at 10.30pm every Friday during term time, and you're guaranteed a robust and entertaining evening.

(☎0131-629 0430; www.bedlamtheatre.co.uk; 11b Bristo Pl; admission £5; 🚌2, 23, 27, 41, 42)

Jazz Bar
JAZZ, BLUES

36 ⭐ Map p36, E4

This atmospheric cellar bar, with its polished parquet floors, bare stone walls, candlelit tables and stylish steel-framed chairs, is owned and operated by jazz musicians. There's live music every night from 9pm to 3am, and on Saturday from 3pm; as well as jazz, expect bands playing blues, funk, soul and fusion. (www.thejazzbar.co.uk; 1a Chambers St; admission £3-7; ⏰5pm-3am Mon-Fri, 2.30pm-3am Sat & Sun; 📶; 🚌35, 45)

Royal Oak
TRADITIONAL MUSIC

37 ⭐ Map p36, F4

This popular folk music pub is tiny, so get there early (9pm start weekdays, 2.30pm Saturdays) if you want to be sure of a place. Sundays from 4pm to 7pm is open session – bring your own instruments (or a good singing voice).

☑️ **Top Tip**

Music at St Giles

St Giles Cathedral (www.stgilescathedral.org.uk; High St; 🚌23, 27, 41, 42) plays host to a regular and varied program of classical music, including popular lunchtime and evening concerts and organ recitals. The cathedral choir sings at the 10am and 11.30am Sunday services; check the cathedral website for a detailed program.

Armstrong's

(www.royal-oak-folk.com; 1 Infirmary St; ☺11.30am-2am Mon-Sat, 12.30pm-2am Sun; ⊒all South Bridge buses)

Bannerman's   LIVE MUSIC

38 ⭐ Map p36, F3

A long-established music venue – it seems like every Edinburgh student for the last four decades spent half their youth here – Bannerman's straggles through a warren of old vaults beneath South Bridge. It pulls in crowds of students, locals and backpackers alike with live rock, punk and indie bands six nights a week. (www.bannermanslive.co.uk; 212 Cowgate; ☺noon-1am Mon-Sat, 12.30pm-1am Sun; 🛜; ⊒35, 45)

Shopping

Armstrong's   VINTAGE

39 🔒 Map p36, C4

Armstrong's (pictured left) is an Edinburgh fashion institution (established in 1840, no less), a quality vintage clothes emporium offering everything from elegant 1940s dresses to funky 1970s flares. As well as having retro fashion, it's a great place to hunt for 'previously owned' kilts and Harris tweed, or to seek inspiration for that fancy-dress party. (☎0131-220 5557; www.armstrongsvintage.co.uk; 83 Grassmarket; ☺10am-5.30pm Mon-Thu, to 6pm Fri & Sat, noon-6pm Sun; ⊒2)

Royal Mile Whiskies   DRINKS

40 🔒 Map p36, D3

If it's a drap of the cratur ye're after, this place has a selection of single malts in miniature and full-size bottles. There's also a range of blended whiskies, Irish whiskey and bourbon, and you can buy online too. (☎0131-225 3383; www.royalmilewhiskies.co.uk; 379 High St; ☺10am-6pm Mon-Sat, 12.30-6pm Sun mid-Sep–Jun, 12.30-8pm daily Jul–mid-Sep; ⊒23, 27, 41, 42)

Ragamuffin   FASHION & ACCESSORIES

41 🔒 Map p36, G2

Quality Scottish knitwear and fabrics including cashmere from Johnstons of Elgin, Fair Isle sweaters and Harris tweed. (☎0131-557 6007; 278

Canongate; ⊙10am-5pm Mon-Sat, noon-5pm Sun; 🚌35)

Bill Baber
FASHION & ACCESSORIES

42 🔒 Map p36, C4

This family-run designer knitwear studio has been in the business for more than 30 years, producing stylish and colourful creations using linen, merino wool, silk and cotton. (☎0131-225 3240; www.hillbaber.com; 66 Grassmarket; ⊙9am-5.30pm Mon-Sat; 🚌2)

Geoffrey (Tailor) Inc
FASHION & ACCESSORIES

43 🔒 Map p36, F2

Geoffrey can fit you out in traditional Highland dress, or run up a kilt in your own clan tartan. Its offshoot, 21st Century Kilts (p83), offers modern fashion kilts in a variety of fabrics. (☎0131-557 0256; www.geoffreykilts. co.uk; 57-59 High St; ⊙9.30am-6pm Mon-Sat, 10.30am-5.30pm Sun; 🚌35)

Joyce Forsyth Designer Knitwear
FASHION & ACCESSORIES

44 🔒 Map p36, D4

The colourful knitwear on show at this intriguing little shop will drag your ideas about woollens firmly into the 21st century. Ms Forsyth's trademark design is a flamboyant, flared woollen coat (can be knitted to order

🔍 Local Life
Cockburn Street Shops

Cockburn St, curving down from the Royal Mile to Waverley train station, is the heart of Edinburgh's youth shopping scene, lined with quirky independent stores peddling everything from goth gear and body piercings to incense and healing crystals. Here you'll find:

▶ **Cookie** (☎0131-622 7260; www.indie-edinburgh.com; 31 Cockburn St; ⊙10am-6pm; 🚌6) Cute party dresses.

▶ **Old Town Context** (☎0131-629 0534; www.oldtowncontext.co.uk; 42-44 Cockburn St; ⊙10am-6pm Mon-Sat, 11am-5pm Sun; 🚌6) Aladdin's cave of unusual gifts.

▶ **Pie in the Sky** (☎0131-220 1477; www. facebook.com/pieinthesky72; 21 Cockburn St; ⊙10am-6pm; 🚌6) Vintage and alternative fashion.

▶ **Underground Solush'n** (☎0131-226 2242; www.undergroundsolushn.com; 9 Cockburn St; ⊙10am-6pm Mon-Wed, Fri & Sat, 10am-7pm Thu, noon-6pm Sun; 🚌6) New and secondhand vinyl; one of the city's best record shops.

in colours of your own choice), but there are also box jackets, jumpers, hats, scarves and shawls. (☎0131-220 4112; www.joyceforsyth.co.uk; 42 Candlemaker Row; ⊙10am-5.30pm Mon-Sat; 🚌2, 23, 27, 41, 42, 45)

Explore

Holyrood & Arthur's Seat

Facing the imposing royal palace of Holyroodhouse at the foot of the Royal Mile, a once near-derelict district has been transformed by the construction of the Scottish Parliament Building. Holyrood Park, a former hunting ground of Scottish monarchs centred on the miniature mountain of Arthur's Seat, allows Edinburghers to enjoy a little bit of wilderness in the heart of the city.

The Sights in a Day

☀ Spend the best part of the morning taking a self-guided tour of the **Palace of Holyroodhouse** (p54) before breaking for lunch in the **Café at the Palace** (p55) or at **Hemma** (p63).

☀ If the weather is good, devote the afternoon to exploring Holyrood Park, climbing to the top of **Arthur's Seat** (p61) for a fantastic view of the city and the Firth of Forth. If it's too cold or wet for outdoor exploration, take a tour of the **Scottish Parliament Building** (p56) followed by a visit to **Our Dynamic Earth** (p61).

☾ In summer you could do worse than to end your day at the **Sheep Heid Inn** (p59) for a pub dinner in the beer garden. In winter book a table at **Rhubarb** (p62) and dress up for an evening of divine decadence.

For a local's day in Holyrood & Arthur's Seat, see p58.

◉ Top Sights

Palace of Holyroodhouse (p54)

Scottish Parliament Building (p56)

♡ Local Life

A Walk Through Holyrood Park p(58)

♥ Best of Edinburgh

Views
Arthur's Seat (p61)

Architecture
Scottish Parliament Building (p56)

For Kids
Our Dynamic Earth (p61)

Drinking
Sheep Heid Inn (p59)

Getting There

🚌 **Bus** Lothian Buses 6 and 35 both run to Holyrood, 35 via the lower half of the Royal Mile and 6 via Holyrood Rd. Bus 42 runs along Duddingston Rd West, a short walk from Duddingston Village, while 4, 5, 15, 26, 44 and 45 run along London Rd, near the north entrance to Holyrood Park.

Top Sights
Palace of Holyroodhouse

The Palace of Holyroodhouse is the royal family's official residence in Scotland, but it is probably most famous as the 16th-century home of the ill-fated Mary, Queen of Scots. She spent six turbulent years here from 1561 to 1567, during which time she debated with John Knox, married her second and third husbands, and witnessed the murder of her secretary, David Rizzio.

👁 Map p60, B1

www.royalcollection.org.uk

Horse Wynd

adult/child incl audioguide £12/7.20

🕘9.30am-6pm Apr-Oct, to 4.30pm Nov-Mar; 📶

🚍6, 35

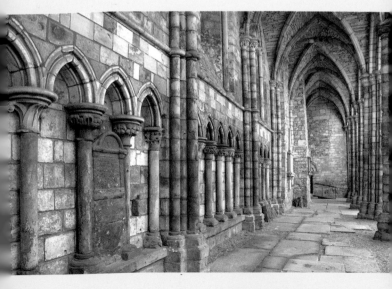

Great Gallery

A self-guided audio tour leads you through a series of impressive royal apartments, ending in the Great Gallery. The 89 portraits of Scottish kings (both real and legendary) were commissioned by Charles II and supposedly record his unbroken lineage from Scota, the Egyptian pharaoh's daughter who discovered the infant Moses in a reed basket on the banks of the Nile.

Mary's Bedchamber

The highlight of the tour is Mary, Queen of Scots' bedchamber, home to the unfortunate Mary from 1561 to 1567 (it's connected to her husband's bedchamber by a secret stairway). It was here that her jealous second husband, Lord Darnley, restrained the pregnant queen while his henchmen murdered her secretary – and favourite – David Rizzio; a plaque in the neighbouring room marks the spot where he bled to death.

Holyrood Abbey

Admission to the palace includes a guided tour of neighbouring **Holyrood Abbey** (April to October only; pictured left), founded by King David I in 1128. It was probably named after a fragment of the True Cross, on which Christ was crucified (rood is an old Scots word for cross), said to have been brought back from the Holy Land by his mother, St Margaret. Most of the surviving ruins date from the 12th and 13th centuries; the royal burial vault holds the remains of kings David II, James II and James V, and of Mary, Queen of Scots' husband Lord Darnley.

☑ **Top Tips**

▶ The palace is closed to the public when the royal family is visiting and during state functions (usually in mid-May, and mid-June to early July); check the website for exact dates.

▶ You can wander through the palace at your own speed; an audioguide is included in the price of admission. Allow at least one to 1½ hours.

▶ If you plan to visit the Queen's Gallery as well, you can buy a combined ticket.

✗ **Take a Break**

Café at the Palace
(Mews Courtyard, Queen's Gallery, mains £6-10; 🚻), in the courtyard of the Queen's Gallery, serves soup and snacks.

Hemma (p63) is a short walk away, and does family-friendly food.

Top Sights
Scottish Parliament Building

The Scottish Parliament Building is a spectacular example of modern architecture, designed by Catalan architect Enric Miralles and officially opened by the Queen in 2005. It's an original and idiosyncratic building that caused a great deal of controversy at the time, but now provides a home for the parliament created in the wake of the Scottish devolution referendum of 1997.

👁 Map p60, A1

☎ 0131-348 5200

www.scottish.parliament.uk

Horse Wynd

admission free; 📶

🕑 9am-6.30pm Tue-Thu & 10am-5pm Mon, Fri & Sat in session, 10am-5pm Mon-Sat in recess

🚍 6, 35

The Exterior

The architect Enric Miralles (1955–2000) believed that a building could be a work of art. However, this weird concrete confection has left many people scratching their heads in confusion. What does it all mean? The strange forms of the exterior are all symbolic in some way, from the oddly shaped projecting windows on the west wall (inspired by the silhouette of *Reverend Robert Walker Skating on Duddingston Loch*, one of Scotland's most famous paintings), to the unusual, inverted-L-shaped panels on the facade (representing a curtain being drawn aside, ie open government). Even the ground plan of the whole complex represents a 'flower of democracy rooted in Scottish soil' (best seen looking down from Salisbury Crags).

The Debating Chamber

The **Main Hall**, inside the public entrance, has a low, triple-arched ceiling of polished concrete, like a cave, or cellar, or castle vault. It is a dimly lit space, the starting point for a metaphorical journey from this relative darkness up to the Debating Chamber (sitting directly above the Main Hall), which is, in contrast, a palace of light – the light of democracy. This magnificent chamber (pictured left) is the centrepiece of the parliament, designed not to glorify but to humble the politicians who sit within it. The windows face Calton Hill, allowing Members of Scottish Parliament (MSPs) to look up to its monuments (reminders of the Scottish Enlightenment), while the massive, pointed oak beams of the roof are suspended by steel threads above the MSPs' heads like so many Damoclean swords.

☑ Top Tips

▶ The public areas of the parliament building – the Main Hall, where there is an exhibition, a shop and cafe, and the public gallery in the Debating Chamber – are open to visitors. Tickets are needed for the public gallery – see website for details.

▶ You can also take a free, one-hour guided tour (advance booking recommended).

▶ If you want to see the parliament in session, check the website for sitting times. Business days are normally Tuesday to Thursday year-round.

✖ Take a Break

There is a cafe in the Parliament Building at the rear of the Main Hall, and another across the street in the Queen's Gallery.

Local Life
A Walk Through Holyrood Park

Holyrood Park covers 650 acres of varied landscape, including crags, moorland and lochs, plus the miniature mountain of Arthur's Seat, little changed since its enclosure as a royal hunting ground in the 16th century. It's a wildlife haven and a huge recreational resource for the city, thronged with walkers, cyclists and picnickers on sunny weekends.

❶ St Margaret's Loch

Begin at the park's northern entrance on Duke's Walk, which leads to St Margaret's Loch, an artificial pond created during Victorian times. The loch is well known for its huge flocks of swans and ducks (please don't feed them – human food is not healthy for wild animals).

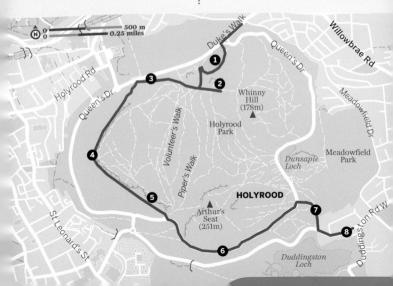

❷ St Anthony's Chapel

Take the path on the south side of the loch and climb up to the ruins of St Anthony's Chapel. Dating from the 15th century, its origins are obscure; it may have been associated with a hospital in Leith donated by King James I (for the treatment of the skin disease erysipelas, also known as St Anthony's Fire), or it may have been a beacon for ships in the Firth of Forth.

❸ St Margaret's Well

Descend back to the road where you'll find St Margaret's Well, a beautiful, late-15th-century Gothic well-house. It was moved, stone by stone, to this location in 1860 when its original site in Meadowbank was taken over by a railway depot. You can't get into the chamber – all you can do is peek at the ornate vaulting through the metal grille at the entrance.

❹ Radical Road

The park's most dramatic feature is the long, curving sweep of Salisbury Crags, a russet curtain of columnar basaltic cliffs. The stony path along the foot of the crags is known as the Radical Road – it was built in 1820, at the suggestion of Sir Walter Scott, to give work to unemployed weavers (from whose politics it took its name).

❺ Hutton's Section

At the southern end of the crags, look out for an interpretation board set in a boulder marking Hutton's Section.

Edinburgh's most famous rock outcrop was used by the pioneering geologist James Hutton in 1788 to bolster his theory that the basaltic rocks of Salisbury Crags were formed by the cooling of molten lava.

❻ Queen's Drive

Continue onto Queen's Dr, built in the 19th century as a scenic carriage drive for Queen Victoria and Prince Albert during their stays at Holyroodhouse. Closed to motor vehicles on Sundays, the drive winds across the southern slopes of Arthur's Seat, with grand views over the city to the Pentland Hills.

❼ Jacob's Ladder

Where the road curves sharply to the north (left), a (signposted) footpath on the right leads to Jacob's Ladder, a steep staircase of 209 steps that descends to the western edge of Duddingston Village.

❽ Duddingston Village

The picturesque little village of Duddingston dates from the 12th century, though only the church survives from that era; most of the houses were built in the 18th century, including the village pub, the **Sheep Heid Inn** (p63), a good place to stop for lunch or a pint. Nearby is **Prince Charlie's Cottage**, where the Young Pretender held a council of war before the Battle of Prestonpans in 1745.

A   B   C   D

Calton
New Burial
Ground

Queen's
Gallery

**Palace of
Holyroodhouse**

1

Canongate
(Royal Mile)

Abbeyhill

Horse
Wynd

4

St Margaret's
Loch

Reid's Cl

**Scottish
Parliament Building**

Queen's Dr

200 m
0.1 miles

Duke's Walk

Holyrood Rd

7

Queen's Dr

2

Our Dynamic
Earth

Queen's Dr

Queen's Dr

2

Volunteer's Walk

Holyrood
Park

Queen's Dr

3

Radical Road

Piper's Walk

1 *Arthur's
Seat*

Arthur's
Seat
(251m)

For reviews see

⦿ Top Sights	p54
◉ Sights	p61
✖ Eating	p62
🍷 Drinking	p63

4

Dalkeith Rd

Holyrood Park Rd

University of
Edinburgh
Pollock Halls
of Residence

Prestonfield
Golf Course

Queen's Dr

5

5

6

3

LONELY PLANET/GETTY IMAGES ©

Our Dynamic Earth

Sights

Arthur's Seat

VIEWPOINT

1 ◎ Map p60, D4

The rocky peak of Arthur's Seat (251m), carved by ice sheets from the deeply eroded stump of a long-extinct volcano, is a distinctive feature of Edinburgh's skyline. The view from the summit is well worth the walk, extending from the Forth Bridges in the west to the distant conical hill of North Berwick Law in the east, with the Ochil Hills and the Highlands on the northwestern horizon. You can hike from Holyrood to the summit in around 45 minutes (Holyrood Park; 🚌6, 35)

Our Dynamic Earth

EXHIBITION

2 ◎ Map p60, A2

Housed in a modernistic white marquee, Our Dynamic Earth (pictured above) is billed as an interactive, multimedia journey of discovery through Earth's history from the Big Bang to the present day. Hugely popular with kids of all ages, it's a slick extravaganza of whiz-bang special effects and 3D movies cleverly designed to fire up young minds with curiosity about all things geological and environmental. Its true purpose, of course, is to disgorge you into a gift shop where you can buy model dinosaurs and souvenir T-shirts. (www.dynamicearth.co.uk; Holyrood Rd;

adult/child £13.50/9; ⏱10am-5.30pm Easter-Oct, to 6pm Jul-Aug, 10am-5.30pm Wed-Sun Nov-Easter, last admission 90min before closing; ♿; 🚌6, 35)

Duddingston Parish Church   CHURCH

3 ⊙ Map p60, D5

Poised on a promontory overlooking Duddingston Loch, this church is one of the oldest buildings in Edinburgh, with some interesting medieval relics at the kirkyard gate: the **Joug**, a metal collar that was used, like the stocks, to tether criminals and sinners, and the **Loupin-On Stane**, a stone step to help gouty and corpulent parishioners get onto their horses. The early-19th-century **watchtower** inside the gate was built to deter body-snatchers.

🔍 Local Life
Urban Hillwalking on Arthur's Seat

To climb Arthur's Seat from Holyrood, cross Queen's Dr and follow the path that slants leftwards up the hillside from the north end of Salisbury Crags, heading towards the ruins of St Anthony's Chapel, then turn south on a rough path that follows the floor of a shallow dip just east of Long Row crags. The path eventually curves around to the left and rises more steeply up some steps to a saddle; turn right here and climb to the rocky summit of Arthur's Seat.

(www.duddingstonkirk.co.uk; Old Church Lane; ⏱church 1-4pm Thu & 2-4pm Sun Aug only, kirkyard dawn-dusk; 🚌42)

Queen's Gallery   GALLERY

4 ⊙ Map p60, B1

This stunning modern gallery, which occupies the shell of a former church and school, is a showcase for exhibitions of art from the Royal Collections. The exhibitions change every six months or so; for details of the latest, check the website. (www.royalcollection.org.uk; Horse Wynd; adult/child £6.70/3.40, combined admission to gallery & Holyroodhouse £16.90/9.50; ⏱9.30am-6pm Apr-Oct, to 4.30pm Nov-Mar; 🚌6, 35)

Eating

Rhubarb   SCOTTISH £££

5 🍴 Map p60, A5

Set in the splendid 17th-century **Prestonfield hotel** (☎0131-668 3346; www.prestonfield.com; Priestfield Rd; r/ste from £285/361; 🅿🛜), Rhubarb is a feast for the eyes as well as the taste buds. The over-the-top decor of rich reds set off with black and gold and the sensuous surfaces – damask, brocade, marble, gilded leather – that make you want to touch everything are matched by the intense flavours and rich textures of the modern Scottish cuisine. (☎0131-225 1333; Prestonfield, Priestfield Rd; mains £18-35; ⏱noon-2pm Mon-Sat, 12.30-3pm Sun, 6-10pm daily)

Understand
Mystery of the Miniature Coffins

In July 1836 some boys hunting for rabbits on the slopes of Arthur's Seat made a strange discovery: in a hollow beneath a rock, arranged on a pile of slates, were 17 tiny wooden coffins. Each was just 4 inches (10cm) long and contained a roughly carved human figure dressed in handmade clothes.

Many theories have been put forward in explanation, but the most convincing is that the coffins were made in response to the infamous Burke and Hare murders of 1831–32: the number of coffins matched the number of known victims. It was a common belief that people whose bodies had been dissected by anatomists could not enter heaven, and it is thought that someone fashioned the tiny figures in order to provide the murder victims with a form of Christian burial.

Eight of the 17 coffins survive, and can be seen in the National Museum of Scotland (p30). Edinburgh author Ian Rankin makes use of the story of the coffins in his detective novel *The Falls*.

Drinking

Sheep Heid Inn   PUB

6 📍 Map p60, D5

Possibly the oldest inn in Edinburgh (with a licence dating back to 1360) the Sheep Heid feels more like a country pub than an Edinburgh bar. Set in the semirural shadow of Arthur's Seat, it's famous for its 19th-century skittles alley and the lovely little beer garden. (www.thesheepheidedinburgh.co.uk; 43-45 The Causeway; ⏱11am-11pm Mon-Thu, to midnight Fri & Sat, noon-11pm Sun; 🚻; 🚌42)

Hemma   BAR

7 📍 Map p60, A2

Set among the glass-and-steel architecture of the redeveloped Holyrood district, Hemma (Swedish for 'at home') is one of a stable of Scandinavian bars, a funky fish-tank of a place furnished with comfy armchairs and sofas and brightly coloured wooden chairs. Good coffee and cakes during the day, real ale and cocktails in the evening. (📞0131-629 3327; www.bodabar.com/hemma; 75 Holyrood Rd; ⏱11am-midnight Mon-Thu, to 1am Fri & Sat, 10am-10pm Sun; 📶🚻; 🚌6)

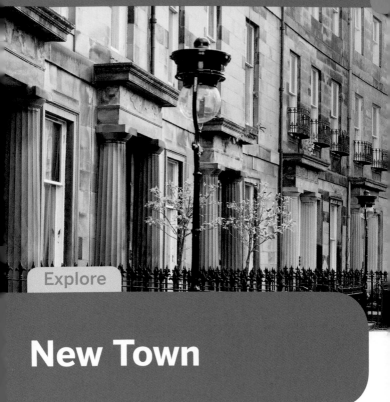

Explore

New Town

Edinburgh's New Town is the world's most complete and unspoilt example of Georgian architecture (pictured above) and town planning; along with the Old Town, it was declared a Unesco World Heritage Site in 1995. Princes St is one of Britain's most spectacular shopping streets, with unbroken views of the castle, while George St is lined with designer boutiques, trendy bars and upmarket restaurants.

The Sights in a Day

☀️ Begin the day with a stroll through the western part of **Princes Street Gardens** (p68), and plan on spending the rest of the morning admiring the art at the **Scottish National Gallery** (p74) and the **Royal Scottish Academy** (p75) before enjoying a Scottish-themed lunch at the gallery's **Scottish Cafe & Restaurant** (p69).

☀️ Continue through the eastern part of the gardens, or along Princes St, to St Andrew Sq and another bout of art appreciation at the **Scottish National Portrait Gallery** (p66). Browse the boutiques in nearby Multrees Walk, or explore the independent shops along George St, Thistle St and Rose St, before climbing **Calton Hill** (p76) for a magnificent sunset view.

🌙 Relax with a cocktail at **Bramble** (p81) before getting a taxi to **Gardener's Cottage** (p77) or **21212** (p79) for an unforgettable dinner (be sure to book in advance), then catch some live jazz at **Jam House** (p82) or a comedy act at **Stand** (p82).

For a local's day in the New Town, see p70.

👁 Top Sights

Scottish National Portrait Gallery (p66)

Princes Street Gardens (p68)

🔍 Local Life

New Town Shopping (p70)

🖤 Best of Edinburgh

Shopping

Jenners (p70)

Harvey Nichols (p71)

Eating

Gardener's Cottage (p77)

Dogs (p77)

Drinking

Café Royal Circle Bar (p80)

Bramble (p81)

Getting There

🚌 **Bus** Just about every bus service in Edinburgh runs along Princes St at some point in its journey. But note that not all buses stop at every bus stop – if you're looking for a particular bus, check the route numbers listed on the bus-stop sign.

🚋 **Tram** The tram line runs from the West End along Princes St to York Pl.

Top Sights
Scottish National Portrait Gallery

The renovated Venetian Gothic palace of the Scottish National Portrait Gallery reopened its doors in 2011, emerging as one of the city's top attractions. Its galleries illustrate Scottish history through paintings, photographs and sculptures, putting faces to Scotland's famous names, from Robert Burns, Mary, Queen of Scots and Bonnie Prince Charlie to actor Sean Connery, comedian Billy Connolly and poet Jackie Kay.

👁 Map p72, D3

www.nationalgalleries.org

1 Queen St

admission free; ♿

🕙 10am-5pm

🚇 St Andrew Sq

Architecture

The museum's exterior is a neo-Gothic froth of friezes, pinnacles and sculptures – the niches at 1st-floor level hold statues of Scottish kings and queens, philosophers and poets, artists and scientists. Mary, Queen of Scots is in the middle of the east wall on North St Andrew St, while the main entrance is framed by Robert the Bruce and William Wallace.

Great Hall

The gallery's interior is decorated in Arts and Crafts style, nowhere more splendidly than in the Great Hall (pictured left). Above the Gothic colonnade a processional frieze painted by William Hole in 1898 serves as a visual encyclopedia of famous Scots, shown in chronological order from Calgacus (the chieftain who led the Caledonian tribes into battle against the Romans) to writer and philosopher Thomas Carlyle (1795–1881). The murals on the 1st-floor balcony depict scenes from Scottish history, while the ceiling is painted with the constellations of the night sky.

Bonnie Prince Charlie

Contrast the 1750 portrait of a dashing Prince Charles Edward Stuart (1720–88), in a tartan suit and Jacobite bonnet, at a time when he still had hopes of returning to Scotland to claim the throne, and the one painted towards the end of his life – exiled in Rome, an alcoholic, a broken man.

Three Oncologists (2002)

This eerie portrait of three leading cancer specialists by Ken Currie somehow captures the horror of the disease, along with the sense that their achievements in treating it are a kind of alchemical mystery.

☑ Top Tips

▶ The gallery's selection of 'trails' leaflets provide a bit of background information while leading you around the various exhibits; the Hidden Histories trail is particularly interesting.

▶ Free guided tours of the gallery's architecture are held at 2pm on the third Saturday of the month; book in advance by calling ☎0131-624 6560.

✕ Take a Break

The excellent soups and sandwiches at the gallery's **Cafe Portrait** (mains £6-10; ⏲10am-4.30pm Fri-Wed, to 6pm Thu; ☏) make it a popular lunch spot for local office workers.

If that's too crowded, head a block west to Dogs (p77) for top nosh at great-value prices.

Top Sights
Princes Street Gardens

The beautiful Princes Street Gardens are slung between Edinburgh's Old and New Towns, and split in the middle by the Mound – around two million cart-loads of earth were dug out from foundations during the construction of the New Town and dumped here to provide a road link across the valley to the Old Town. It was completed in 1830.

👁 Map p72, B5

Princes St

admission free

🕑 dawn–dusk

🚌 all Princes St buses

Scott Monument

The eastern half of Princes Street Gardens is dominated by the massive Gothic spire of the **Scott Monument** (www.edinburghmuseums.org.uk; East Princes Street Gardens; admission £5; 10am-7pm Apr-Sep, 10am-4pm Oct-Mar; Princes St), built by public subscription in memory of the novelist Sir Walter Scott after his death in 1832. The exterior is decorated with carvings of characters from his novels, inside you can see an exhibition on Scott's life, and climb the 287 steps to the top for a superb view of the city.

West End Churches

The western end of the gardens is dominated by the tower of **St John's Church**, worth visiting for its fine Gothic Revival interior. It overlooks **St Cuthbert's Parish Church**, built in the 1890s on a site of great antiquity – there has been a church here since at least the 12th century, and perhaps since the 7th century. There is a circular **Watch Tower** in the graveyard, a reminder of the days when graves had to be guarded against body-snatchers.

Floral Clock & Ross Bandstand

At the entrance to the western gardens on the corner of Princes St and the Mound is the Floral Clock, a working clock laid out in flowers; it was first created in 1903 and the design changes every year. In the middle of the western part of the gardens is the Ross Bandstand, a venue for open-air concerts in summer and at Hogmanay, and the stage for the famous Fireworks Concert during the Edinburgh Festival (there are plans to replace the ageing bandstand with a modern concert venue).

☑ Top Tips

▶ The gardens are home to events throughout the year, from the Edinburgh Festival Fireworks Concert to the Christmas Market and ice-skating rink in December.

▶ Spring is the time to see the flower displays at their best – in April the slopes below the castle esplanade are thick with yellow daffodils.

▶ On Saturday you can buy food from the Farmers Market on Castle Tce, then grab a bench in the neighbouring gardens for an alfresco meal.

✕ Take a Break

The **Scottish Cafe & Restaurant** (0131-226 6524; www.thescottish-cafeandrestaurant.com; The Mound; mains £13-15; 9am-5.30pm Fri-Wed, to 7pm Thu;), beneath the Royal Scottish Academy (p75), offers the chance to enjoy traditional Scottish cuisine with a view along the eastern gardens.

Local Life
New Town Shopping

Shopping in the New Town offers everything from mall-crawling and traditional department stores to browsing in dinky little designer boutiques and rubbing shoulder-bags with fussing fashionistas in Harvey Nicks. And all in a compact city centre that you can cover without blowing the bank on taxis or getting blisters from your Blahniks.

❶ Jenners

Founded in 1838, **Jenners** (www.houseof-fraser.co.uk; 48 Princes St; ◷9.30am-6.30pm Mon-Wed, 8am-9pm Thu, 8am-8pm Fri, 8am-7pm Sat, 11am-6pm Sun) is the grande dame of Edinburgh shopping. Its five floors stock a wide range of quality goods, both classic and contemporary (it's especially strong on designer shoes and handbags, hats, knitwear and oriental rugs) plus a food hall, hairdresser, gift-wrapping service and four cafes.

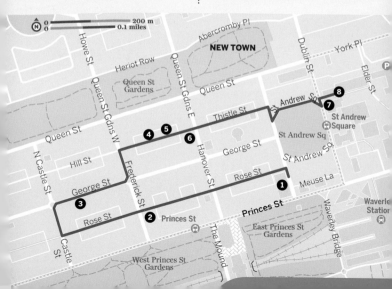

❷ Rose Street

Pedestrianised Rose St was once notorious as a pub crawl; there are still pubs, but the street is better known today for shops, mostly mainstream, which range from outdoor sports emporiums such as Cotswold Outdoor and Tiso to antique jewellery specialists like **Alistir Wood Tait** (www.alistirtaitgem.co.uk; 116a Rose St; ⏰10.30am-5.30pm Tue-Fri, 9.30am-5pm Sat).

❸ Cruise

An ornately corniced foyer leads into three floors of minimalist gallery-like decor. This **branch** (www.cruisefashion.co.uk; 94 George St; ⏰9.30am-6pm Mon-Wed & Fri, 10am-7pm Thu, 9am-6pm Sat, 11am-6pm Sun) and an outlet at nearby 80 George St show off the best of mainstream designer labels including Paul Smith, Jasper Conran, Hugo Boss, Joseph Tricot, Armani and Dolce & Gabbana.

❹ Kakao by K

Thistle St, Rose St's partner to the north of George St, has become an enclave of designer boutiques. **Kakao by K** (www.kakao.co.uk; 45 Thistle St; ⏰10am-6pm Mon-Sat year-round, noon-4pm Sun Dec) is typical, a showcase for Scandinavian fashion labels such as Fillipa K and House of Lykke, as well as handbags, scarves and even jewellery designed by the shop's Danish owner.

❺ Alchemia

Made in a workshop in Fife, the jewellery on display at **Alchemia** (www.alchemia.co.uk; 37 Thistle St; ⏰10.30am-5.30pm Tue-Sat) is designed in Scotland and inspired by the shapes and colours of the natural world. If nothing catches your eye, you can request bespoke jewellery – former clients have included royalty.

❻ Covet

Another Thistle St stalwart, **Covet** (www.thoushaltcovet.com; 20 Thistle St; ⏰10am-6pm Mon-Sat, noon-5pm Sun) has an emphasis on up-and-coming new designers from all over the world. Look for bags by Dutch label Smaak and New York designer Rebecca Minkoff, jewellery by Tatty Devine, and watches from Swedish brand Triwa.

❼ Harvey Nichols

The jewel in the crown of Edinburgh's shopping scene, **Harvey Nichols** (www.harveynichols.com; 30-34 St Andrew Sq; ⏰10am-6pm Mon-Wed, 10am-8pm Thu, 10am-7pm Fri & Sat, 11am-6pm Sun) has four floors of designer labels and is the anchor for the Multrees Walk luxury shopping mall. Nearby you'll find boutiques by Louis Vuitton, Mulberry, Hugo Boss, Swarovski and more.

❽ Valvona & Crolla VinCaffè

By now you'll be looking forward to a break; **VinCaffè** (www.valvonacrolla.co.uk; 11 Multrees Walk, St Andrew Sq; mains £9-19; ⏰7.30am-7pm Mon-Wed, to 9pm Thu-Sat, 10am-7pm Sun; 📶🍴) is an ideal place for lunch, or perhaps just a bottle of pink pinot grigio shared over a platter of antipasti.

A
B
C
D

STOCKBRIDGE
Edinburgh Academy
Eyre Pl
King George V Park

1
Henderson Row
Fettes Row
Royal Cres
Scotland St

Dean Bank La
Hamilton Pl
W Silvermills La
Clarence St
Cumberland St
Dundonald St
Drummond Pl

St Stephen St
St Vincent St
Circus La
Great King St
Dublin St

2
Kerr St
NW Circus Pl
Circus Pl
Howe St
Dundas St
Northumberland St

India Pl
India St
Royal Circus
29 🔒

Dean Gardens
Gloucester La
Jamaica Mews
Heriot Row
Abercromby Pl
Scottish National Portrait Gallery

Moray Pl
Queen St Gdns W
Queen St Gardens
Queen St Gdns E
Queen St
25 ☆

3
10 ❌
12 ❌ 19 ❌
Thistle St
St Andrew S

33 🔒
16

George St
31 🔒

St Colme St
Hill St
Hanover St
Rose St

4
Young St
22 🍴
N Castle St
11 🍴
Frederick St

◉ **Georgian House** 3
24 🍴
George St
32 🔒
Princes St 🚇
Royal Scottish Academy ◉ 2
East Princes S Gardens

◉ **4 Charlotte Square**
Castle St
The Mound

Rose St
Princes St

5
Hope St
S Charlotte St

◉ **Princes Street Gardens**
West Princes St Gardens
◉ 1 **Scottish National Gallery**
N Bank St

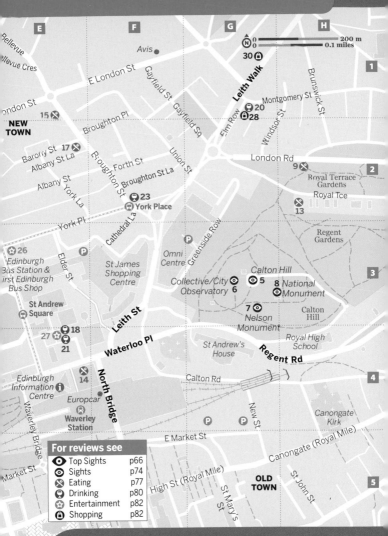

Understand
New Town History

Between the end of the 14th century and the start of the 18th, the population of Edinburgh – still confined within the walls of the Old Town – increased from 2000 to 50,000. The tottering tenements were unsafe and occasionally collapsed, fire was an ever-present danger and the overcrowding and squalor became unbearable. There was no sewer system and household waste was disposed of by flinging it from the window into the street with a euphemistic shout of 'Gardyloo!' (from the French 'gardez l'eau' – beware of the water). Passersby replied with 'Haud yer haun'!' (Hold your hand) but were often too late. The stink that rose from the streets was ironically referred to as 'the floo'rs o' Edinburgh' (the flowers of Edinburgh).

So when the *Act of Union* in 1707 brought the prospect of long-term stability, the upper classes wanted healthier, more spacious living quarters, and in 1766 the Lord Provost of Edinburgh announced a competition to design an extension to the city. It was won by an unknown 23-year-old, James Craig, a self-taught architect whose elegant plan envisaged the New Town's main axis, George St, following the crest of a ridge to the north of the Old Town, with grand squares at each end. Building was restricted to just one side of Princes St and Queen St, so that the houses had views over the Firth of Forth to the north, and to the castle and Old Town to the south.

During the 18th and 19th centuries, the New Town continued to sprout squares, circuses, parks and terraces, with some of its finest neoclassical architecture designed by Robert Adam. Today it is one of the world's finest examples of a Georgian cityscape, and is part of a Unesco World Heritage Site.

Sights

Scottish National Gallery
GALLERY

1 ⊙ Map p72, D5

Designed by William Playfair, this imposing classical building with its Ionic porticoes dates from the 1850s. Its octagonal rooms, lit by skylights, have been restored to their original Victorian decor of deep-green carpets and dark-red walls. The gallery houses an important collection of European art from the Renaissance to post-Impressionism, with works by Verrocchio (Leonardo da Vinci's teacher), Tintoretto, Titian, Holbein, Rubens, Van Dyck, Vermeer, El Greco, Poussin, Rembrandt, Gainsborough, Turner, Constable, Monet, Pissarro, Gauguin and Cézanne. (www.nationalgalleries.org; The Mound; fee for special exhibitions varies; ☉10am-5pm Fri-Wed, to 7pm Thu; 🛜; 🚌Princes St)

Royal Scottish Academy GALLERY

2 ◉ Map p72, D4

This Greek Doric temple, with its northern pediment crowned by a seated figure of Queen Victoria, is the home of the Royal Scottish Academy. Designed by William Playfair and built between 1823 and 1836, it was originally called the Royal Institution; the RSA took over the building in 1910. The galleries display a collection of paintings, sculptures and architectural drawings by academy members dating from 1831, and they also host temporary exhibitions throughout the year. (☏0131-225 6671; www.royalscottishacademy.org; The Mound; fee for special exhibitions varies; ☉10am-5pm Mon-Sat, noon-5pm Sun; ☏; ☐Princes St)

Bute House, Charlotte Square

Georgian House HISTORIC BUILDING

3 ◉ Map p72, A4

The National Trust for Scotland's Georgian House has been beautifully restored and furnished to show how Edinburgh's wealthy elite lived at the end of the 18th century. The walls are decorated with paintings by Allan Ramsay, Sir Henry Raeburn and Sir Joshua Reynolds, and there's a fully equipped 18th-century kitchen complete with china closet and wine cellar. (NTS; www.nts.org.uk; 7 Charlotte Sq; adult/child £7/5.50; ☉10am-6pm Jul & Aug, 10am-5pm Apr-Jun & Sep-Oct, 11am-4pm Mar & Nov; ☐36, 47)

Charlotte Square SQUARE

4 ◉ Map p72, A4

At the western end of George St is Charlotte Sq, the architectural jewel of the New Town, which was designed by Robert Adam shortly before his death in 1791. The northern side of the square is Adam's masterpiece and one of the finest examples of Georgian architecture anywhere. **Bute House** (pictured above), in the centre at No 6, is the official residence of Scotland's first minister. (☐19, 36, 37, 41, 47)

Calton Hill
VIEWPOINT

5 Map p72, G3

Calton Hill (100m), which rises dramatically above the eastern end of Princes St, is Edinburgh's acropolis, its summit scattered with grandiose memorials dating mostly from the first half of the 19th century. It is also one of the best viewpoints in Edinburgh, with a panorama that takes in the castle, Holyrood, Arthur's Seat, the Firth of Forth, New Town and the full length of Princes St. (🚌 all Leith St buses)

Collective/City Observatory
GALLERY

6 Map p72, G3

The design of the City Observatory, built in 1818, was based on the ancient Greek Temple of the Winds in Athens. Its original function was to provide a precise, astronomical time-keeping service for marine navigators, but smoke from Waverley train station forced the astronomers to move to Blackford Hill in the south of Edinburgh in 1895. It has been redeveloped as a stunning space for contemporary visual art, and opened to the public for the first time in its history. (📞 0131-556 1264; www.collectivegallery.net; Calton Hill; admission free; 🕙 10am-5pm Tue-Sun Apr-Jul & Sep, to 4pm Oct-Mar, to 6pm daily Aug; 🚌 all Leith St buses)

Nelson Monument
MONUMENT

7 Map p72, G3

Looking a bit like an upturned telescope – the similarity is intentional – and offering superb views over the city and across the Firth of Forth, the Nelson Monument was built to commemorate Admiral Lord Nelson's victory at Trafalgar in 1805. (www.edinburghmuseums.org.uk; Calton Hill; admission £5; 🕙 10am-7pm Mon-Sat, noon-5pm Sun Apr-Sep, 10am-3pm Mon-Sat Oct-Mar; 🚌 all Leith St buses)

National Monument
MONUMENT

8 Map p72, G3

The largest structure on the summit of Calton Hill, the National Monument was a rather over-ambitious attempt to replicate the Parthenon in Athens, and was intended to honour Scotland's dead in the Napoleonic

---

Local Life
Edinburgh Zoo

Opened in 1913, **Edinburgh Zoo** (www.edinburghzoo.org.uk; 134 Corstorphine Rd; adult/child £19/14.55; 🕙 9am-6pm Apr-Sep, to 5pm Oct & Mar, to 4.30pm Nov-Feb; 👶) is one of the world's leading conservation zoos. Edinburgh's captive breeding program has helped save many endangered species, including Siberian tigers, pygmy hippos and red pandas. The main attractions are the two giant pandas, Tian Tian and Yang Guang, who arrived in December 2011 and the penguin parade (the zoo's penguins go for a walk every day at 2.15pm).

Understand
The One O'Clock Gun

On Princes St you can tell locals and visitors apart by their reaction to the sudden explosion that rips through the air each day at one o'clock. Locals check their watches, while visitors shy like startled ponies. It's the One O'Clock Gun, fired from Mills Mount Battery on the castle battlements at 1pm sharp every day except Sunday.

The gun's origins date from the mid-19th century, when the accurate setting of a ship's chronometer was essential for safe navigation. The city authorities installed a time-signal on top of the Nelson Monument that was visible to ships anchored in the Firth of Forth. The gun was added as an audible signal that could be used when rain or mist obscured the visual signal. An interesting little exhibition in the Museum of Edinburgh (p38) details the gun's history and workings.

Wars. Construction – paid for by public subscription – began in 1822 but funds ran dry when only 12 columns had been erected. It became known locally as 'Edinburgh's Disgrace'. (Calton Hill; 🚌all Leith St buses)

Eating

Gardener's Cottage SCOTTISH ££

9 🍽 Map p72, H2

This country cottage in the heart of the city, bedecked with flowers and fairy lights, offers one of Edinburgh's most interesting dining experiences – two tiny rooms with communal tables made of salvaged timber, and a menu based on fresh local produce (most of the vegetables and fruit are grown in a local organic garden). Bookings essential; brunch served

at weekends. (📞0131-558 1221; www.thegardenerscottage.co; 1 Royal Terrace Gardens, London Rd; lunch mains £16-17, dinner set menu £40; ⏰noon-2pm & 5-10pm Mon & Wed-Fri, 10am-2pm & 5-10pm Sat & Sun; 🚌all London Rd buses)

Dogs BRITISH ££

10 🍽 Map p72, C3

One of the coolest tables in town, this bistro-style place uses cheaper cuts of meat and less well-known, more sustainable species of fish to create hearty, no-nonsense dishes such as devilled kidneys on toast; shredded lamb with skirlie (fried oatmeal and onion), pomegranate seeds and almonds; and beetroot and horseradish spelt risotto. (📞0131-220 1208; www.thedogsonline.co.uk; 110 Hanover St; mains lunch £6, dinner £9-22; ⏰noon-2.30pm & 6-10pm Mon-Fri, noon-4pm & 6-10pm Sat & Sun; 🍴; 🚌23, 27)

Understand

Literary Edinburgh

- -

Sir Walter Scott

The writer most deeply associated with Edinburgh is undoubtedly Sir Walter Scott (1771–1832), Scotland's greatest and most prolific novelist, best remembered for classic tales such as *The Antiquary, The Heart of Midlothian, Ivanhoe, Redgauntlet* and *Castle Dangerous*. He lived at various New Town addresses before moving to his country house at Abbotsford.

Robert Louis Stevenson

Robert Louis Stevenson (1850–94) was born at 8 Howard Pl, in the New Town, into a family of famous lighthouse engineers. Stevenson is known and loved around the world for stories such as *Kidnapped, Catriona, Treasure Island, The Master of Ballantrae* and *The Strange Case of Dr Jekyll and Mr Hyde,* many of which have been made into successful films. The most popular and enduring is *Treasure Island* (1883), which has been translated into many different languages and has never been out of print.

Muriel Spark

No list of Edinburgh novelists would be complete without mention of Dame Muriel Spark (1918–2006), who was born in Edinburgh and educated at James Gillespie's High School for Girls, an experience that provided material for her best-known novel *The Prime of Miss Jean Brodie* (1961), a shrewd portrait of 1930s Edinburgh. Dame Muriel was a prolific writer; her 22nd novel, *The Finishing School,* was published in 2004 when she was 86.

Contemporary Writers

Walk into any bookshop in Edinburgh and you'll find a healthy 'Scottish Fiction' section, with recently published works by best-selling Edinburgh authors such as Candia McWilliam, Ian Rankin, Sara Sheridan, Alexander McCall Smith and Irvine Welsh.

Ian Rankin's Rebus novels are dark, engrossing mysteries that explore the darker side of Scotland's capital city, filled with sharp dialogue, telling detail and three-dimensional characters. Although she was born in England, the publishing phenomenon that is JK Rowling famously began her career by penning the first Harry Potter adventure while nursing a coffee in various Edinburgh cafes; she still lives in Scotland.

Contini

ITALIAN ££

11 🍽 Map p72, B4

A palatial Georgian banking hall enlivened by fuchsia-pink banners and lampshades is home to this lively, child-friendly Italian bar and restaurant, where the emphasis is on fresh, authentic ingredients (produce imported weekly from Milan; home-made bread and pasta) and uncomplicated enjoyment of food. (📞0131-225 1550; www.contini.com/contini-ristorante; 103 George St; mains £11-30; ⏱7.30am-11pm Mon-Fri, 9am-midnight Sat, 9am-11pm Sun; 📶🍴♿; 🚌all Princes St buses)

Urban Angel

CAFE ££

12 🍽 Map p72, C3

A wholesome deli that puts the emphasis on fair-trade, organic and locally sourced produce, Urban Angel is also a delightfully informal cafe-bistro that serves all-day brunch (porridge with honey, French toast, eggs Benedict), tapas and a wide range of light, snacky meals. (📞0131-225 6215; www.urban-angel.co.uk; 121 Hanover St; mains £6-13; ⏱8am-5pm Mon-Fri, 9am-5pm Sat & Sun; 🍴♿; 🚌23, 27)

21212

FRENCH £££

13 🍽 Map p72, H2

A grand Georgian town house on the side of Calton Hill is the elegant setting for one of Edinburgh's Michelin stars. Divine decor by Timorous Beasties and Ralph Lauren provide the backdrop to an exquisitely prepared five-course dinner (£70 a head) that changes weekly and features fresh, seasonal delights such as baby turbot poached in olive oil with saffron pancake, and lamb and merguez kebab with banana and cucumber confit. (📞0131-523 1030; www.21212restaurant. co.uk; 3 Royal Tce; 3-course lunch/dinner £32/55; ⏱noon-1.45pm & 7-9pm Tue-Sat; 📶; 🚌all London Rd buses)

Hadrian's Brasserie

SCOTTISH, FRENCH ££

14 🍽 Map p72, E4

The brasserie at the **Balmoral Hotel** (📞0131-556 2414; www.thebalmoralhotel. com; 1 Princes St; s/d from £277/299; 🅿📶🏊) has a 1930s art-deco feel, with pale-green walls, dark-wood furniture, and waiters dressed in white aprons and black waistcoats. The menu includes posh versions of popular dishes such as fish and chips, haggis with whisky sauce, and rump steak with Café de Paris sauce. (📞0131-557 5000; www.roccofortehotels.com; Balmoral Hotel, 1 Princes St; mains £15-22; ⏱7-10.30am, noon-2.30pm & 5.30-10pm Mon-Fri, 7.30-11am & 12.30-10.30pm Sat & Sun; ♿; 🚌all Princes St buses)

L'Escargot Bleu

FRENCH ££

15 🍽 Map p72, E1

As with its sister restaurant, L'Escargot Blanc (p90) on Queensferry St, this cute little bistro is as Gallic as garlic but makes fine use of quality Scottish produce – the French-speaking staff will lead you knowledgeably through a menu that includes authentic Savoyard *tartiflette, quenelle* of pike with lobster sauce, and pigs' cheeks braised in red wine. Two-course lunch/early-bird menu £12.90. (📞0131-557 1600; www.lescargotbleu.co.uk; 56 Broughton St; mains £13-19; ⏰noon-2.30pm & 5.30-10pm Mon-Thu, noon-3pm & 5.30-10.30pm Fri & Sat; 👶; 🚌8)

Fishers in the City
SEAFOOD ££

16 ✖ Map p72, C4

This more sophisticated version of the famous Fishers Bistro (p109) in Leith, with granite-topped tables, split-level dining area and nautical theme, specialises in superior Scottish seafood – the knowledgeable staff serve up plump and succulent oysters, meltingly sweet scallops, and sea bass that's been grilled to perfection. (📞0131-225 5109;

Local Life
Bohemian Broughton

The lively, bohemian district of Broughton, centred on Broughton St at the northeastern corner of the New Town, is the focus of Edinburgh's gay scene and home to many good bars, cafes and restaurants. **CC Blooms** (Map p73, G2; 📞0131-556 9331; http://ccbloomsedinburgh.com; 23 Greenside Pl; ⏰11am-3am Mon-Sat, 12.30pm-3am Sun; 📶; 🚌all Leith Walk buses), opposite the top end of Broughton St, is the city's biggest gay club.

www.fishersbistros.co.uk; 58 Thistle St; mains £17-23; ⏰noon-10.30pm Mon-Sat, 12.30-10.30pm Sun; 📶👶; 🚌13, 19, 37, 41)

Broughton Deli
CAFE £

17 ✖ Map p72, E2

Mismatched cafe tables and chairs in a bright back room behind the deli counter provide an attractive setting for brunch just off the main drag of the New Town's bohemian Broughton St. Brunch is served till 2pm weekdays or 3pm on weekends; choose from American-style pancakes, veggie fry-ups, and poached eggs on toast with organic smoked salmon. (📞0131-558 7111; www.broughton-deli.co.uk; 7 Barony St; mains £6-10; ⏰8am-7pm Mon-Fri, 9am-6pm Sat, 10am-5pm Sun; 📶👶👶; 🚌8)

Drinking

Café Royal Circle Bar
PUB

18 🍺 Map p72, E4

Perhaps *the* classic Edinburgh pub, the Café Royal's main claims to fame are its magnificent oval bar and its Doulton tile portraits of famous Victorian inventors. Sit at the bar or claim one of the cosy leather booths beneath the stained-glass windows, and choose from the seven real ales on tap. (www.caferoyaledinburgh.co.uk; 17 West Register St; ⏰11am-11pm Mon-Wed, to midnight Thu, to 1am Fri & Sat, 12.30-11pm Sun; 📶; 🚌Princes St)

Bramble
COCKTAIL BAR

19 Map p72, C3

One of those places that easily earns the sobriquet 'best-kept secret', Bramble is an unmarked cellar bar where a maze of stone and brick hideaways conceals what is arguably the city's best cocktail venue. No beer taps, no fuss, just expertly mixed drinks. (📞0131-226 6343; www.bramblebar.co.uk; 16a Queen St; ⏱4pm 1am; 🚌23, 27)

Joseph Pearce's
PUB

20 Map p72, G1

This traditional Victorian pub has been remodelled and given a new lease of life by the Swedish owners. It's a real hub of the local community with good food (very family friendly before 5pm), a relaxed atmosphere, and events like Monday night Scrabble games and August crayfish parties. (📞0131-556 4140; www.bodabar.com/joseph-pearces; 23 Elm Row; ⏱11am-midnight Sun-Thu, to 1am Fri & Sat; 🛜👶; 🚌all Leith Walk buses)

Guildford Arms
PUB

21 Map p72, E4

Located in a side alley off the east end of Princes St, the Guildford is a classic Victorian pub full of polished mahogany, brass and ornate cornices. The range of real ales is excellent – try to get a table in the unusual upstairs gallery, with a view over the sea of drinkers below. (📞0131-556 4312; www.

Top Tip

Bus Info on Your Phone

Lothian Buses has created free smartphone apps that provide route maps, timetables and live waiting times for city buses. Search for EdinBus (iPhone), My Bus Edinburgh (Android) or BusTracker Edinburgh (Windows Phone).

guildfordarms.com; 1 West Register St; 🛜; 🚌Princes St)

Oxford Bar
PUB

22 Map p72, A4

The Oxford is that rarest of things: a real pub for real people, with no 'theme', no music, no frills and no pretensions. 'The Ox' has been immortalised by Ian Rankin, author of the Inspector Rebus novels, whose fictional detective is a regular here. Occasional live folk music. (📞0131-539 7119; www.oxfordbar.co.uk; 8 Young St; ⏱11am-midnight Mon-Sat, 12.30-11pm Sun; 🛜; 🚌19, 36, 37, 41, 47)

Mathers
PUB

23 Map p72, F2

Mathers is a friendly, relaxed neighbourhood pub with Edwardian decor serving real ales and good pub grub, with football and rugby matches on the TV. (📞0131-556 6754; www.matherseastend.co.uk; 25 Broughton St; ⏱9am-midnight Mon-Thu, to 1am Fri-Sun; 🛜; 🚌York Pl)

Tigerlily
COCKTAIL BAR

24 🍸 Map p72, A4

Swirling textured wallpapers, glittering chain-mail curtains, crystal chandeliers, and plush pink and gold sofas have won a cluster of design awards for this boutique hotel bar, where sharp suits and stiletto heels line the banquettes. There's expertly mixed cocktails, as well as Czech Staropramen beer on draught, and Innis & Gunn Scottish ale in bottles. (☎0131-225 5005; www.tigerlilyedinburgh.co.uk; 125 George St; ⏰11am-1am; 🛜; 🚌all Princes St buses)

Lulu
CLUB

Lush leather sofas, red satin cushions, fetishistic steel-mesh curtains and dim red lighting all help to create a decadent atmosphere in this drop-dead-gorgeous club venue (see 24 🍸 Map p72, A4) beneath the **Tigerlily boutique hotel** (www.tigerlilyedinburgh.co.uk; from £175; 🛜). Resident and guest DJs show a bit more originality than your average club. (☎0131-225 5005; www.luluedinburgh.co.uk; 125 George St; ⏰10pm-3am; 🛜; 🚌all Princes St buses)

Entertainment

Jam House
LIVE MUSIC

25 ⭐ Map p72, D3

The brainchild of rhythm-and-blues pianist and TV personality Jools Holland, the Jam House is set in a former BBC TV studio and offers a combination of fine dining and live jazz and blues performances. Admission is for over-21s only, and there's a smart-casual dress code. (☎0131-220 2321; www.thejamhouse.com; 5 Queen St; admission from £4; ⏰6pm-3am Fri & Sat; 🚌10, 11, 12, 16, 26, 44)

Stand Comedy Club
COMEDY

26 ⭐ Map p72, E3

The Stand, founded in 1995, is Edinburgh's main independent comedy venue. It's an intimate cabaret bar with performances every night and a free Sunday lunchtime show. (☎0131-558 7272; www.thestand.co.uk; 5 York Pl; tickets £2-15; ⏰from 7.30pm Mon-Sat, from 12.30pm Sun; 🚌St Andrew Sq)

Voodoo Rooms
LIVE MUSIC

27 ⭐ Map p72, E4

Decadent decor of black leather, ornate plasterwork and gilt detailing create a funky setting for this complex of bars and performance spaces above the Café Royal that host everything from classic soul and Motown to Vegas lounge club nights (www.vegasscotland.co.uk) and live local bands. (☎0131-556 7060; www.thevoodoorooms.com; 19a West Register St; admission free-£10; ⏰noon-1am Fri-Sun, 4pm-1am Mon-Thu; 🚌St Andrew Sq)

Shopping

Valvona & Crolla
FOOD & DRINKS

28 🔒 Map p72, G1

The acknowledged queen of Edinburgh delicatessens, established during the

1930s, Valvona & Crolla is packed with Mediterranean goodies, including an excellent choice of fine wines. It also has a good cafe. (☎0131-556 6066; www.valvonacrolla.co.uk; 19 Elm Row; ⏱8.30am-6pm Mon-Thu, 8am-6.30pm Fri & Sat, 10am-5pm Sun; ☐all Leith Walk buses)

Scottish Gallery ARTS & CRAFTS

29 🔒 Map p72, C2

Home to Edinburgh's leading art dealers, Aitken Dott, this private gallery exhibits and sells paintings by contemporary Scottish artists and the masters of the late 19th and early 20th centuries (including the Scottish Colourists), as well as a wide range of ceramics, glassware, jewellery and textiles. (☎0131-558 1200; www.scottish-gallery.co.uk; 16 Dundas St; ⏱10am-6pm Mon-Fri, to 4pm Sat; ☐23, 27)

McNaughtan's Bookshop BOOKS

30 🔒 Map p72, G1

The maze of shelves at McNaughtan's bookshop – established in 1957 – houses a broad spectrum of general second-hand and antiquarian books, with good selections of Scottish, history, travel, art and architecture, and children's books. (☎0131-556 5897; www.mcnaughtansbook-shop.com; 3a-4a Haddington Pl, Leith Walk; ⏱11am-5pm Tue-Sat; ☐all Leith Walk buses)

Fopp MUSIC

31 🔒 Map p72, D4

A good place to hunt for cheap CDs and vinyl, and the friendly staff really know what they're talking about.

✓ Top Tip

Late Shopping Days

Most shops in Edinburgh open late on Thursdays, till 7pm or 8pm. Many city-centre stores extend their late opening to all weekdays during the Edinburgh Festival in August, and during the three weeks before Christmas.

(☎0131-220 0310; www.fopp.com; 3-15 Rose St; ⏱9am-6pm Mon-Sat, 11am-6pm Sun; ☐all Princes St buses)

Palenque JEWELLERY

32 🔒 Map p72, B4

Palenque is a treasure trove of contemporary silver jewellery and handcrafted accessories made using ceramics, textiles and metal-work. (☎0131-225 7194; www.palenquejewellery.co.uk; 99 Rose St; ⏱9.30am-5.30pm Mon-Sat, 11am-5pm Sun; ☐Princes St)

21st Century Kilts FASHION & ACCESSORIES

33 🔒 Map p72, C4

21st Century Kilts offers modern fashion kilts in a variety of fabrics; celebrity customers include Robbie Williams and Vin Diesel. (http://21stcenturykilts.com; 48 Thistle St; ⏱10am-6pm Tue-Sat; ☐23, 27)

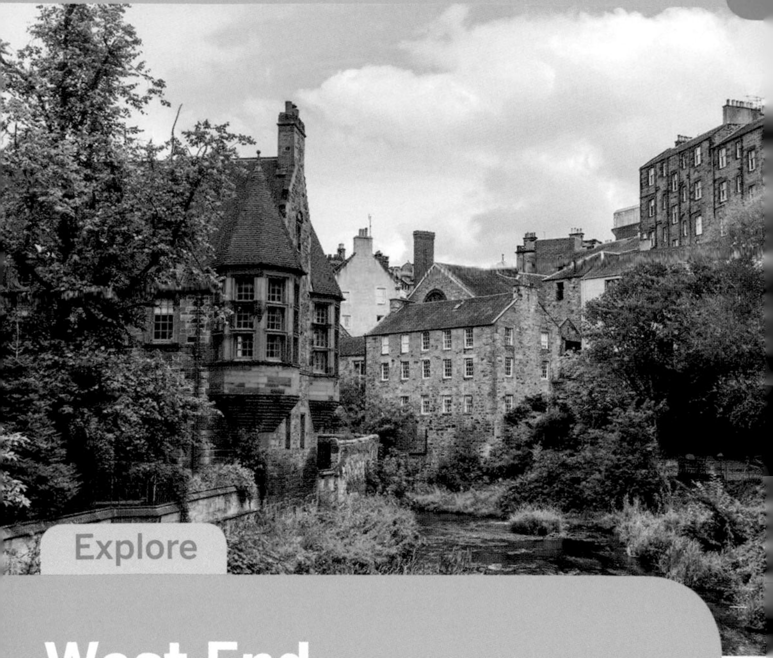

Explore

West End
& Dean Village

Edinburgh's West End is an extension of the New Town, with elegant Georgian terraces, garden squares and an enclave of upmarket shops along William St and Stafford St. It takes in the Exchange district, now the city's financial powerhouse; and the theatre quarter on Lothian Rd; and in the west tumbles downhill into the valley of the Water of Leith to meet the picturesque Dean Village (pictured above).

The Sights in a Day

☀ Enjoy breakfast with the newspapers at **Indigo Yard** (p91), then take a stroll among the fashion boutiques of Stafford St and William St before heading down to **Dean Village** (p89). Follow the Water of Leith Walkway upstream to the **Scottish National Gallery of Modern Art** (p86), and plan on having lunch at **Cafe Modern One** (p87).

☀ Spend the afternoon admiring the modern masterpieces at the gallery's two major exhibition spaces – don't forget to allow time to explore the outdoor sculptures and landscape art in the gallery grounds. Then head back uphill to the West End via Belford Rd and Palmerston Pl for a relaxing pint of real ale at **Bert's Bar** (p92).

☾ Book a pre-theatre dinner – at **Kanpai** (p90) for sushi, or **L'Escargot Blanc** (p90) for French cuisine – and then take in a performance at the **Traverse** (p92) or **Royal Lyceum** (p92) theatre. Or, if you'd prefer some traditional Scottish entertainment, go for dinner and a *ceilidh* (evening of traditional Scottish music and dancing) at the **Ghillie Dhu** (p91).

👁 Top Sights

Scottish National Gallery of Modern Art (p86)

💜 Best of Edinburgh

Eating

Castle Terrace (p90)

Timberyard (p90)

McKirdy's Steakhouse (p91)

Shopping

Edinburgh Farmers Market (p90)

Museums & Galleries

Scottish National Gallery of Modern Art (p86)

Getting There

🚌 **Bus** Lothian Buses 3, 4, 12, 25, 26, 31, 33 and 44 head west from Princes St to the West End, going along Shandwick Pl to Haymarket. For Dean Village, take bus 19, 36, 37, 41 or 47 from George St to Dean Bridge and walk down Bell's Brae.

Top Sights
Scottish National Gallery of Modern Art

Edinburgh's gallery of modern art is split between two impressive neoclassical buildings surrounded by landscaped grounds. As well as showcasing a stunning collection of paintings by the popular, post-Impressionist Scottish Colourists, the gallery is the starting point for a walk along the Water of Leith, following a trail of sculptures by Antony Gormley.

👁 Map p88, A2

www.nationalgalleries.org

75 Belford Rd

fee for special exhibitions varies

🕙10am-5pm

🚌13

Modern One

The main collection, known as Modern One, concentrates on 20th-century art, with various European movements represented by the likes of Matisse, Picasso, Kirchner, Magritte, Miró, Mondrian and Giacometti. American and English artists are also represented, but most space is given to Scottish painters – from the Scottish Colourists of the early 20th century to contemporary artists such as Peter Howson and Ken Currie.

Modern Two

Directly across Belford Rd from Modern One, another neoclassical mansion (formerly an orphanage) houses its annexe, Modern Two, home to a large collection of sculpture and graphic art created by Edinburgh-born artist Sir Eduardo Paolozzi. One of the 1st-floor rooms houses a re-creation of Paolozzi's studio, while the rest of the building stages temporary exhibitions of modern art.

The Grounds

The surrounding grounds feature sculptures by Henry Moore, Rachel Whiteread, Julian Opie and Barbara Hepworth, among others, as well as a sensuous landform artwork by Charles Jencks, and the *Pig Rock Bothy*, a rustic timber performance and exhibition space created in 2014 as part of the Bothy Project (www.thebothyproject.org).

Water of Leith

A footpath and stairs at the rear of the gallery lead down to the Water of Leith Walkway. This takes you past *6 Times*, a sculptural project by Antony Gormley consisting of five human figures standing at various points along the river (the sixth sprouts from the pavement at the gallery entrance). The river statues are designed to fall over in flood conditions, so some of them may not be visible after heavy rain.

☑ Top Tips

▶ A free shuttle bus runs between here and the Scottish National Gallery on the Mound (p74), with hourly departures from 11am to 5pm.

▶ The Scottish National Galleries' website offers a fascinating online game called Artist Rooms (www.national-galleries.org/collection/artist-rooms-game) which enables you to put together and share your own virtual art exhibition.

✗ Take a Break

Cafe Modern One (mains £4-8; ⏱9am-4.30pm Mon-Fri, 10am-4.30pm Sat & Sun; 🛜♿) has an outdoor terrace overlooking the sculptures in the grounds.

Cafe Modern Two (72 Belford Rd; mains £6-8; ⏱10am-4.30pm Mon-Sat, 11am-4.30pm Sun; 🛜♿) is based on a belle époque Viennese coffee house. Both serve cakes and coffee, plus hot lunch dishes from noon till 2.30pm.

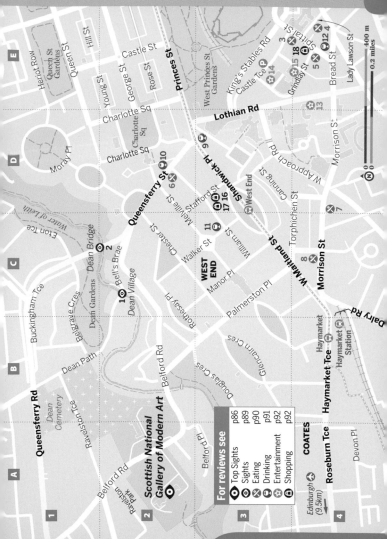

Princes St

Lothian Rd

Queensferry St

Shandwick Pl

W Maitland St

Morrison St

Haymarket Tce

Roseburn Tce

West End

WEST END

COATES

Dean Village

Dean Bridge

Scottish National
Gallery of Modern Art

Heriot Row

Queen St
Gardens

Queen St

Hill St

Castle St

George St

Rose St

Charlotte Sq

Charlotte Sq

Charlotte
Sq

Young St

Moray Pl

Bell's Brae

Dean Gardens

Chester St

Melville St

Stafford St

Walker St

William St

Manor Pl

Rothesay Pl

Palmerston Pl

Glencairn Cres

Douglas Cres

Belford Rd

Belford Pl

Dean Path

Buckingham Tce

Belgrave Cres

Eton Tce

Water of Leith

Queensferry Rd

Dean
Cemetery

Ravelston Tce

Ravelston Park

Belford Rd

King's Stables Rd

Castle Tce

West Princes St
Gardens

Castle St

Spittal St

Bread St

Lady Lawson St

Grindlay St

Morrison St

Canning St

W Approach Rd

Torphichen St

Haymarket
Station

Haymarket Tce

Dalry Rd

Devon Pl

Edinburgh
(9.5km)

N

0   400 m
0   0.2 miles

For reviews see

🔷	Top Sights	p86
🔵	Sights	p89
✖	Eating	p90
✖	Drinking	p91
✪	Entertainment	p92
✖	Shopping	p92

HELENA SMITH/GETTY IMAGES ©

Dean Bridge

Sights

Dean Village AREA

1 ◎ Map p88, C2

Set in the valley that runs beneath the Dean Bridge ('dene' is a Scots word for valley), Dean Village was founded as a milling community by the canons of Holyrood Abbey in the 12th century and by 1700 there were 11 water mills here, grinding grain for flour. One of the old mill buildings has been converted into flats, and the village is now an attractive residential area, with walkways along the river. (🚊19, 36, 37, 41, 47)

Dean Bridge BRIDGE

2 ◎ Map p88, C2

Designed by Thomas Telford and built between 1829 and 1832 to allow the New Town to expand to the northwest, the Dean Bridge (pictured above) vaults gracefully over the narrow, steep-sided valley of the Water of Leith. It soon became notorious as a suicide spot – it soars 27m above the river – and in 1912 the parapets were raised to deter jumpers. (🚊19, 36, 37, 41, 47)

Eating

Castle Terrace

SCOTTISH £££

3 🍴 Map p88, E3

It was little more than a year after opening in 2010 that Castle Terrace was awarded a Michelin star under chef-patron Dominic Jack. The menu is seasonal and applies sharply whetted Parisian skills to the finest of local produce, be it Ayrshire pork, Aberdeenshire lamb or Newhaven crab – even the cheese in the sauces is Scottish. (📞0131-229 1222; www.castle-terracerestaurant.com; 33-35 Castle Tce; 3-course lunch/dinner £29.50/65; ⏰noon-2.15pm & 6.30-10pm Tue-Sat; 🚌2)

Timberyard

SCOTTISH £££

4 🍴 Map p88, E4

Ancient worn floorboards, cast-iron pillars, exposed joists, and tables

🔵 Local Life
Edinburgh Farmers Market

Every Saturday, against the impressive backdrop of the castle crags, the city's **farmers market** (Map p88, E3; 📞0131-652 5940; www.edinburghfarmersmarket.com; Castle Tce; ⏰9am-2pm Sat; 🚌all Lothian Rd buses) is lined with stalls selling everything from heather honey to handmade cheeses, home-reared venison, smoked trout, seasonal wild game, and organic eggs from rare-breed hens.

made from slabs of old mahogany create a rustic, retro atmosphere in this slow-food restaurant where the accent is on locally sourced produce from artisan growers and foragers. Typical dishes include seared scallop with apple, Jerusalem artichoke and sorrel; and juniper-smoked pigeon with wild garlic flowers and beetroot. (📞0131-221 1222; www.timberyard.co; 10 Lady Lawson St; 4-course lunch or dinner £55; ⏰noon-2pm & 5.30-9.30pm Tue-Sat; 📶♿; 🚌2, 35)

Kanpai Sushi

JAPANESE ££

5 🍴 Map p88, E4

What is probably Edinburgh's best sushi restaurant impresses with its minimalist interior, fresh, top-quality fish and elegantly presented dishes – the squid tempura comes in a delicate woven basket, while the sashimi combo is presented as a flower arrangement in an ice-filled stoneware bowl. (📞0131-228 1602; www.kanpaisushi.co.uk; 8-10 Grindlay St; mains £9-15, sushi per piece £4-10; ⏰noon-2.30pm & 5-10.30pm Tue-Sun; 🚌all Lothian Rd buses)

L'Escargot Blanc

FRENCH ££

6 🍴 Map p88, D2

This superb neighbourhood bistro, with French chef and waitstaff, and two-thirds of its top quality produce sourced in Scotland (one-third imported from France), is a true 'Auld Alliance' of culinary cultures. Choose from a menu of classics such as *escargots* in garlic, parsley and hazelnut butter; *coq au vin* (made with free-range Scottish chicken); and perfectly prepared Scottish rib-eye steak with *bleu d'Auvergne* sauce. (☎0131-226 1890; www.lescargotblanc.co.uk; 17 Queensferry St; 3-course lunch/dinner £13.90/25; ☺noon-2.30pm & 5.30-10pm Mon-Thu, noon-3pm & 5.30-10.30pm Fri & Sat; ♦; ☐19, 36, 37, 41, 47)

McKirdy's Steakhouse
SCOTTISH ££

7 ✕ Map p88, D4

The McKirdy brothers – owners of a local butcher business established in 1895 – have cut out the middleman and now run one of Edinburgh's best steakhouses. The friendly staff here serve up starters – such as haggis with Drambuie sauce – and juicy, perfectly cooked steaks, from rump to T-bone, accompanied by mustard mash or crispy fries. There's a kids' menu, and you can get a two-course early dinner (until 6.30pm) for £14. (☎0131-229 6660; www.mckirdyssteak-house.co.uk; 151 Morrison St; mains £11-29; ☺5.30-10pm Sun-Thu, 5-10.30pm Fri & Sat; �♦; ☐2)

Chop Chop
CHINESE £

8 ✕ Map p88, C4

Chop Chop is a Chinese restaurant with a difference, in that it serves dishes popular in China rather than Britain – as its slogan says, 'Can a billion people be wrong?' No sweet-and-sour pork here, but a range of delicious dumplings filled with pork and coriander, beef and chilli, or lamb and leek, and unusual vegetarian dishes such as aubergine fried with garlic and Chinese spices. (☎0131-221 1155; www.chop-chop.co.uk; 248 Morrison St; mains £6-12; ☺noon-2pm & 5.30-10pm Mon-Sat, Sun 12.30-2.30pm & 5-10pm; ✏; ☐Haymarket)

Drinking

Ghillie Dhu
PUB

9 ☕ Map p88, D3

This spectacular bar, with its huge, chunky beer hall tables, leather sofa booths, and polished black-and-white tile floor makes a grand setting for the live folk music sessions that take place here every night (from 10pm, admission free). (☎0131-222 9930; www.ghillie-dhu.co.uk; 2 Rutland Pl; ☺11am-3am Mon-Fri, 10am-3am Sat & Sun; ☐all Princes St buses)

Indigo Yard
BAR

10 ☕ Map p88, D2

Set around an airy, stone-floored and glass-roofed courtyard, Indigo Yard is a fashionable West End watering hole that has been patronised by the likes of Liam Gallagher, Pierce Brosnan and Kylie Minogue. Good food – including open-air barbecues during the summer months – just adds to the attraction. (☎0131-220 5603; www.indigoyardedinburgh.co.uk; 7 Charlotte Lane; ☺8am-1am; audio♦; ☐19, 36, 37, 41, 47)

Bert's Bar
PUB

11 Map p88, C3

A classic re-creation of a 1930s-style pub – a welcoming womb with warm wood and leather decor, complete with a jar of pickled eggs on the bar – Bert's is a good place to sample real ale and down-to-earth pub grub such as Scotch pies and bangers and mash. (0131-225 5748; 29-31 William St; 10am-midnight Sun-Thu, to 1am Fri & Sat; ; West End)

Blue Blazer
PUB

12 Map p88, E4

With its mosaic floors, polished gantry, cosy fireplace and efficient bar staff, the Blue Blazer is a down-to-earth antidote to the designer excess of modern-style bars, catering to a loyal clientele of real-ale enthusiasts, rum aficionados (it's home to the Edinburgh Rum Club) and Saturday horse-racing fans. (0131-229 5030; www.theblueblazer.co.uk; 2 Spittal St; 11am-1am Mon-Sat, 12.30pm-1am Sun; ; 2, 35)

Entertainment

Filmhouse
CINEMA

13 Map p88, E4

The Filmhouse is the main venue for the annual **Edinburgh International Film Festival** (www.edfilmfest.org.uk) and screens a full program of art-house, classic, foreign and second-run films, with lots of themes, retrospectives and 70mm screenings. It has wheelchair access to all three screens. (0131-228 2688; www.filmhousecinema.com; 88 Lothian Rd; ; all Lothian Rd buses)

Traverse Theatre
THEATRE

14 Map p88, E3

The Traverse is the main focus for new Scottish writing and stages an adventurous program of contemporary drama and dance. The box office is only open on Sunday (from 4pm) when there's a show on. (0131-228 1404; www.traverse.co.uk; 10 Cambridge St; box office 10am-6pm Mon-Sat, to 8pm show nights; ; all Lothian Rd buses)

Royal Lyceum Theatre
THEATRE

15 Map p88, E4

A grand Victorian theatre located beside the Usher Hall, the Lyceum stages drama, concerts, musicals and ballet. (0131-248 4848; www.lyceum.org.uk; 30b Grindlay St; box office 10am-6pm Mon-Sat, to 8pm show nights; ; all Lothian Rd buses)

Shopping

Studio One
GIFTS & SOUVENIRS

16 Map p88, D3

This Georgian basement filled with quality homewares, toys, bags, scarves, candles and kitchenware is a godsend for anyone looking to buy that special birthday or Christmas gift. (0131-226 5812; www.studio-one.co.uk; 10 Stafford St; 10am-6pm Mon-Wed, Fri & Sat, to 7pm Thu, 11am-5pm Sun; West End)

Edinburgh Farmers Market (p90)

Liam Ross JEWELLERY

17 🔒 Map p88, D3

Distinctive, hand-crafted jewellery is the hallmark of goldsmith Liam Ross. Choose from the range of gorgeous rings, bracelets and pendants on display, or commission a bespoke item from the man himself. (📞0131-225 6599; www.jewellerybyliamross.com; 12 William St; ⏱9am-5.30pm Tue-Fri, 10am-5pm Sat; 🚇West End)

McAlister Matheson Music MUSIC

18 🔒 Map p88, E4

This is Scotland's biggest and most knowledgeable shop for classical music CDs, DVDs and books – just about every staff member seems to have a music degree. It also stocks a selection of Scottish folk and Celtic music. (📞0131-228 3827; www.mmmusic.co.uk; 1 Grindlay St; ⏱9.30am-6pm Mon-Fri, 9am-5.15pm Sat; 🚇2, 35)

Explore

Stockbridge

Stockbridge is a bohemian enclave to the north of the city centre, with an interesting selection of shops and a good choice of pubs and neighbourhood bistros. Originally a mill village, it was developed in the early 19th century on lands owned largely by the painter Sir Henry Raeburn, who gave his name to its main street, Raeburn Pl.

The Sights in a Day

☼ The best way to arrive in Stockbridge is by walking along the **Water of Leith**, starting from either Dean Village (10 minutes) or the Scottish National Gallery of Modern Art (25 minutes). Stroll the streets and browse the shops before enjoying lunch at one of the bistros in St Stephen St.

☼ Walk along the cobbled lane of St Bernard's Row, then Arboretum Ave and Arboretum Place to the **Royal Botanic Garden** (p96), and plan to spend the rest of the afternoon exploring its many attractions. Don't forget to grab a coffee at the **Terrace Cafe** (p97) and soak up the view of the castle.

☾ Stockbridge nightlife is decidedly low-key, consisting of tempting restaurants and laid-back bars. Grab a sofa in the **Stockbridge Tap** (p102) to enjoy the best of Scottish real ales.

For a local's day in Stockbridge, see p98.

◉ Top Sights
Royal Botanic Garden (p96)

◐ Local Life
A Sunday Stroll Around Stockbridge (p98)

♥ Best of Edinburgh
Shopping
Galerie Mirages (p103)

Annie Smith (p103)

Stockbridge Market (p99)

Drinking
Stockbridge Tap (p102)

Kay's Bar (p102)

Getting There

🚌 **Bus** Lothian Buses 24, 29 and 42 run from Frederick St in the city centre to Raeburn Pl in Stockbridge. Bus 36 cuts across the neighbourhood from St Bernard's Cres and Leslie Pl to Hamilton Pl and Henderson Row.

Top Sights
Royal Botanic Garden

Edinburgh's Royal Botanic Garden is the second-oldest institution of its kind in Britain (after Oxford's), and one of the most respected in the world. Founded near Holyrood in 1670 and moved to its present location in 1823, it has 70 beautifully landscaped acres that include splendid Victorian glasshouses, colourful swathes of rhododendron and azalea, and a world-famous rock garden.

Map p100, C1

☎ 0131-248 2909

www.rbge.org.uk

Arboretum Pl

admission free

🕐 10am-6pm Mar-Sep, to 5pm Feb & Oct, to 4pm Nov-Jan

🚌 8, 23, 27

John Hope Gateway

The garden's visitor centre is housed in this striking, environmentally friendly building overlooking the main Arboretum Pl entrance. There are exhibitions on biodiversity, climate change and sustainable development, as well as displays of rare plants from the institution's collection and a specially created biodiversity garden.

Glasshouses

A cluster of around 25 glasshouses (admission £5.50) in the garden's northern corner houses a huge collection of tropical plants. Pride of place goes to the ornate Victorian palm house, built in 1834 and home to vast rainforest palms, including a Bermudan palmetto that dates from 1822. The Front Range of 1960s designer glasshouses is famous for its tropical pond filled with giant Amazonian water lilies.

Rock Garden

Since it was first created in 1871, the rock garden has been one of the garden's most popular features. Boulders and scree slopes made from Scottish sandstone and conglomerate are home to more than 4000 species of alpine and subarctic plants from all over the world.

Sculptures

Pick up a map from the visitor centre so that you can track down the garden's numerous sculptures, ranging from a statue of Swedish botanist and taxonomist Carl Linnaeus (1707–78) by Scottish architect Robert Adam, to modern works by Yorkshire sculptor Barbara Hepworth and landscape artist Andy Goldsworthy.

☑ Top Tips

▶ Guided tours of the gardens (per person £5) depart at 11am and 2pm daily from April to October.

▶ The main entrance is the West Gate, on Arboretum Pl; however, city buses stop near the smaller East Gate on Inverleith Row. The Majestic Tour (p144) bus drops off and picks up at the West Gate.

▶ It's worth visiting the website before your visit to check out what the current month's seasonal highlights are.

✕ Take a Break

The **Gateway Restaurant** (☎0131-552 2674; www.gatewayrestaurant.net; John Hope Gateway, Royal Botanic Garden, mains £7-11; ⊙10am-5.15pm) in the John Hope Gateway visitor centre serves hot breakfast and lunch dishes.

The **Terrace Cafe** (☎0131-552 0606; mains £5-8; ⊙10am-5.30pm; 🚶), in the middle of the gardens, has outdoor tables with a superb view of the city skyline.

Local Life
A Sunday Stroll Around Stockbridge

Just a short walk downhill from the city centre, Stockbridge feels a world away with its peaceful back-streets, leafy Georgian gardens, quirky boutiques and art galleries, and the Water of Leith flowing through the middle. There's a strong community spirit that really comes alive on Sundays, when Stockbridge Market attracts crowds of local shoppers and browsers.

① Breakfast at the Botanics
Take bus 8, 23 or 27 to the main entrance to the Royal Botanic Garden on Arboretum Pl, and head for the **Gateway Restaurant** (p97) to enjoy breakfast with a view over the gardens. Choose from filled bagels, eggs Benedict, fruit salad or a full Scottish fry-up.

❷ Stockbridge Colonies

A short walk along Arboretum Pl and Arboretum Ave leads to the Stockbridge Colonies, a series of terraced stone houses built by a workers' co-operative in the 19th century to provide affordable working-class accommodation (now not so affordable). Carved stone plaques on several gable ends show the tools of the tradesmen who built them.

❸ Browse St Stephen Street's shops

This side street is pure Stockbridge, crammed with tiny galleries, boutiques, restaurants and basement bars. **Miss Bizio** (www.missbiziocouture.com) is a cornucopia of high-end vintage fashion, while **Sheila Fleet** (https://sheilafleet.com) is a showcase for the work of the Orkney-based jewellery designer. At St Stephen Pl, you can see the Georgian archway that once led to the old Stockbridge meat market.

❹ Gloucester Lane

This steep, cobbled street was once the main thoroughfare connecting Stockbridge to the city, before the New Town was built. **Duncan's Land**, at the corner with India Pl (now **Nok's Kitchen** (p102) is one of Stockbridge's oldest surviving buildings, dating from 1790, though it used masonry from demolished Old Town buildings (the lintel is dated 1605).

❺ St Bernard's Well

A short walk along the Water of Leith Walkway leads to **St Bernard's Well**

(☉noon-3pm Sun Aug only), a circular temple with a statue of Hygeia, the goddess of health, built in 1789. The sulphurous spring was discovered by schoolboys from **George Heriot's School** (www.george-heriots.com; Lauriston Pl; ☉Sep only) in 1760, and became hugely popular during the late-18th-century fad for 'taking the waters' – one visitor compared the taste to 'the washings of foul gun barrels'.

❻ Ann Strcet

The Georgian garden villas along Ann St (named after Sir Henry Raeburn's wife; 1817) are among the most beautiful and desirable houses in Edinburgh – the street is reckoned to be the most expensive in the city, and was named in 2008 as one of the UK's six most exclusive streets. It is also the setting for JM Barrie's 1902 novel *Quality Street.*

❼ Raeburn Place

Stockbridge's main drag is a bustle of shops, pubs and restaurants, with everything from chain stores and charity shops to craft shops, galleries and jewellery boutiques.

❽ Stockbridge Market

On Sundays, **Stockbridge Market** (www.stockbridgemarket.com; cnr Kerr St & Saunders St; ☉10am-5pm Sun) is the focus of the community, set in a leafy square next to the bridge that gives the district its name. Stalls range from fresh Scottish produce to handmade ceramics, jewellery, soaps and cosmetics. Grab an espresso from Steampunk Coffee, which operates out of a 1970s VW campervan.

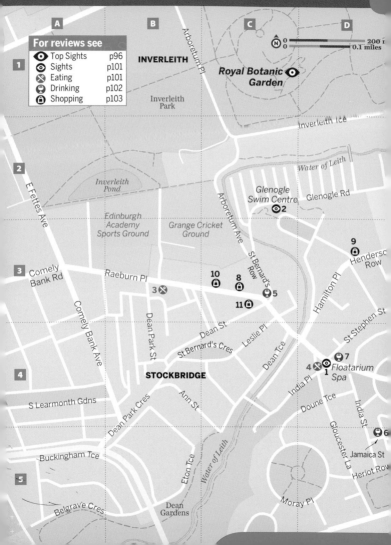

A **B** **C** **D**

For reviews see
◉	Top Sights	p96
◉	Sights	p101
✗	Eating	p101
✜	Drinking	p102
⌂	Shopping	p103

INVERLEITH

Arboretum Pl

N 0 200 m
0 0.1 miles

Royal Botanic ◉
Garden

Inverleith
Park

Inverleith Tce

E Fettes Ave

Water of Leith

Inverleith
Pond

Glenogle
Swim Centre
◉2 Glenogle Rd

Edinburgh
Academy
Sports Ground

Grange Cricket
Ground

Arboretum Ave

9
⌂ Henderso
Row

Comely
Bank Rd

Raeburn Pl

10
⌂

8
⌂

St Bernard's Row

Hamilton Pl

St Stephen St

Comely Bank Ave

3✗

Dean Park St

11⌂

◉5

Dean St

Leslie Pl

St Bernard's Cres

Dean Tce

Dean Park Cres

STOCKBRIDGE

Ann St

India Pl

4✗◉ ✜7
◉1 *Floatarium*
Spa

S Learmonth Gdns

Doune Tce

India St

Buckingham Tce

Eton Tce

Water of Leith

Gloucester La

✜6
Jamaica St

Belgrave Cres

Dean
Gardens

Moray Pl

Heriot Row

Annie Smith jewellery studio (p103)

Sights

Floatarium Spa HEALTH & FITNESS

1 ◉ Map p100, D4

Escape from the bustle of the city centre in a warm, womb-like flotation tank, or enjoy the many other therapies on offer, including facials, aromatherapy massage, reflexology, shiatsu, reiki and Indian head massage (appointments necessary). There's a sweet-scented shop, too, where you can buy massage oils, incense, candles, homeopathic remedies, CDs and so on. (✆0131-225 3350; edinburghfloatarium.co.uk; 29 NW Circus Pl; float per hr £45; ⊙10am-3pm Mon, to 8pm Tue-Fri, to 6pm Sat, to 5pm Sun; ◻24, 29, 42)

Glenogle Swim Centre SWIMMING

2 ◉ Map p100, C2

Atmospheric Victorian swimming baths with a 25m pool, sauna and gym. (✆0131-343 6376; www.edinburghleisure.co.uk; Glenogle Rd; adult/family £5/12.50; ⊙7am-10pm Mon-Fri, 8am-4pm Sat & Sun; ◻36)

Eating

Scran & Scallie GASTROPUB ££

3 ✖ Map p100, B3

Established by the Michelin-starred team responsible for the Kitchin (p109) and Castle Terrace (p90), this laid-back gastropub adds a modern chef's touch to old-time dishes such

Explore

Leith

Leith has been Edinburgh's seaport since the 14th century, but it fell into decay following WWII. It is now undergoing a steady revival, with old warehouses turned into luxury flats and a lush crop of trendy bars and restaurants sprouting up along the waterfront leading to Ocean Terminal, a huge new shopping and leisure complex, and the former Royal Yacht *Britannia*.

The Sights in a Day

☼ Begin your day with a stroll along the **Shore** (p109), Leith's original waterfront. Cross the Water of Leith and follow Ocean Dr to **Ocean Terminal** (p111), where you can spend the rest of the morning aboard the **Royal Yacht Britannia** (p106); don't forget to take tea and scones in the ship's Royal Deck Tea Room.

☼ There are plenty of good lunch spots with outdoor tables at nearby Victoria Dock. **A Room in Leith** (p110) has tables on a pontoon floating in the dock, while you'll need to reserve well ahead to get a table at Michelin-starred the **Kitchin** (p109). In the afternoon, take a leisurely stroll along the seafront past pretty **Newhaven Harbour** (p109) and enjoy a drink or two in the **Old Chain Pier** (p111) pub.

☾ Leith nightlife is more about eating and drinking than culture and entertainment, so – once again – plan in advance to be sure of a dinner table at one of the neighbourhood's top restaurants: **Martin Wishart** (p109) or **Fishers Bistro** (p109). Follow up with cocktails served in a teapot at the **Roseleaf** (p110), or pints of real ale at **Teuchters Landing** (p111).

👁 Top Sights

Royal Yacht *Britannia* (p106)

♥ Best of Edinburgh

Eating
Fishers Bistro (p109)
Martin Wishart (p109)
Kitchin (p109)
Shore (p110)

Drinking
Roseleaf (p110)
Old Chain Pier (p111)
Lioness of Leith (p111)

Shopping
Kinloch Anderson (p111)

Getting There

🚌 **Bus** Lothian Buses 10, 12, 16 and 22 run from Princes St down Leith Walk to the junction of Constitution and Great Junction Sts; from here 10 and 16 go west to Newhaven; 22 goes north to the Shore and Ocean Terminal; and 12 goes east to Leith Links. Buses 11, 34, 35 and 36 also terminate at Ocean Terminal.

Top Sights
Royal Yacht Britannia

Built on Clydeside, the former Royal Yacht *Britannia* was the British royal family's floating holiday home during their foreign travels from the time of her launch in 1953 until her decommissioning in 1997. Now moored permanently in front of Ocean Terminal, a tour of the ship provides an intriguing insight into the queen's private tastes.

👁 Map p108, A1

www.royalyachtbritannia.co.uk

Ocean Terminal

adult/child £15/8.50; 📶

🕑9.30am-6pm Jul-Sep, to 5.30pm Apr-Jun & Oct, 10am-5pm Nov-Mar, last admission 90min before closing

🚌11, 22, 34, 35, 36

State Apartments

The former Royal Yacht *Britannia* is a monument to 1950s decor, and the accommodation reveals Her Majesty's preference for simple, unfussy surroundings. The queen travelled with 45 members of the royal household, five tons of luggage and a Rolls-Royce that was squeezed into a specially built garage on the deck (it's still there). The State Drawing Room, which once hosted royal receptions, is furnished with chintz sofas bolted firmly to the floor, and a baby grand piano where Noël Coward once tickled the ivories.

Royal Bedrooms

The private cabins of the queen and Prince Philip are surprisingly small and plain, with 3ft-wide single beds (the only double bed on board is in the honeymoon suite, used by Prince Charles and Princess Diana in 1981). The thermometer in the queen's bathroom was used to make sure the water was the correct temperature and, when in harbour, one yachtsman was charged with ensuring that the angle of the gangway never exceeded 12 degrees.

On Deck

The Burmese teak decks were scrubbed daily, but all work near the royal accommodation was carried out in complete silence and had to be finished by 8am. Note the mahogany windbreak that was added to the balcony deck in front of the bridge; it was put there to stop wayward breezes from blowing up skirts and revealing the royal undies.

Bloodhound

Britannia was joined in 2010 by the 1930s racing yacht *Bloodhound*, which was owned by the Queen in the 1960s. She is moored alongside *Britannia* (except in July and August, when she is away cruising) as part of an exhibition about the royal family's love of all things nautical.

☑ Top Tips

▶ You tour the ship at your own pace, using an audioguide. You'll need at least two hours to see everything.

▶ The Majestic Tour (p144) bus runs from Waverley Bridge to *Britannia* during opening times.

▶ The Royal Edinburgh Ticket (adult/child £51/28), available from Majestic Tour, gives admission to *Britannia*, Edinburgh Castle and the Palace of Holyroodhouse, plus two days travel on local tour buses.

✕ Take a Break

Britannia's sun deck (now enclosed in glass) makes a stunning setting for the **Royal Deck Tea Room** (mains £5-13; ⏰10am-4.30pm Apr-Oct, 10.30am-4pm Nov-Mar), where you can enjoy coffee and cake, or even a bottle of champagne, with a view across the Firth of Forth to the hills of Fife.

Western
Harbour

A

**Royal Yacht
Britannia**

1

11 🔒

Leith
Docks

B

Ocean Dr

For reviews see
◉	Top Sights	p106
◉	Sights	p109
✕	Eating	p109
🍺	Drinking	p110
🔒	Shopping	p111

C

D

N 0 ──── 200
  0 ──── 0.1 miles

Imperial
Dock

Albert
Dock

Victoria
Dock

2

◀◉2

◀🍺10

Victoria Quay

Commercial Quay

Commercial St

Dock Pl

✕3

🔒12

Dock St

Sandport Pl

8✕

Coburg St

N Junction St

Water of Leith

Tower Pl

◉7

◉5 Tower St

◉The
1 Shore

✕6

Bernard St

Baltic St

3

The Shore

✕4 Water St

Maritime St

Mitchell St

Elbe St

Mill La

Cables Wynd

Great Junction St

Henderson St

Giles St

Tolbooth Wynd

Kirkgate

Constitution St

Queen
Charlotte St

Poplar
La

Links St

4

Bangor Rd

Bonnington Rd

Jane St

Tennant St

Pilrig
Park

Duke St

🍺9

Wellington Pl

Duncan Pl

John's Pl

Leith
Links

5

Sights

The Shore   AREA

1 🎯 Map p108, C3

The most attractive part of Leith is this cobbled waterfront street alongside the Water of Leith, lined with pubs and restaurants. Before the docks were built in the 19th century this was Leith's original wharf. An iron plaque in front of No 30 marks the King's Landing – the spot where King George IV (the first reigning British monarch to visit Scotland since Charles II in 1650) stepped ashore in 1822. (🚌16, 22, 35, 36)

Newhaven Harbour   HARBOUR

2 🎯 Map p108, A2

Newhaven was once a distinctive fishing community whose fishwives tramped the streets of Edinburgh's New Town selling *caller herrin* (fresh herring) from wicker creels on their backs. Modern development has dispelled the fishing-village atmosphere, but the little harbour still boasts its picturesque lighthouse. (Newhaven Pl; 🚌7, 11,16)

Eating

Kitchin   SCOTTISH £££

3 🍴 Map p108, B3

Fresh, seasonal, locally sourced Scottish produce is the philosophy that has won a Michelin star for this elegant but unpretentious restaurant. The menu

moves with the seasons, of course, so expect fresh salads in summer and game in winter, and shellfish dishes such as baked scallops with white wine, vermouth and herb sauce when there's an 'r' in the month. (📞0131-555 1755; http://thekitchin.com/; 78 Commercial Quay; 3-course lunch/dinner £30/70; 🕐12.15-2.30pm & 6.30-10pm Tue-Thu, to 10.30pm Fri & Sat; 🅿; 🚌16, 22, 35, 36)

Martin Wishart   FRENCH £££

4 🍴 Map p108, C3

In 2001 this restaurant became the first in Edinburgh to win a Michelin star, and has retained it ever since. The eponymous chef has worked with Albert Roux, Marco Pierre White and Nick Nairn, and brings a modern French approach to the best Scottish produce, from langoustines with kohlrabi, vanilla and passionfruit, to a six-course vegetarian tasting menu. (📞0131-553 3557; www.martin-wishart.co.uk; 54 The Shore; 3-course lunch/dinner £29/75; 🕐noon-2pm & 7-10pm Tue-Fri, noon-1.30pm & 7-10pm Sat; 🅿; 🚌16, 22, 35, 36)

Fishers Bistro   SEAFOOD ££

5 🍴 Map p108, C2

This cosy little restaurant, tucked beneath a 17th-century signal tower, is one of the city's best seafood places. The menu ranges widely in price, from cheaper dishes such as classic fish cakes with lemon and chive mayonnaise to more expensive delights such as North Berwick lobster thermidor. (📞0131-554

5666; www.fishersbistros.co.uk; 1 The Shore; mains £12-25; ⊙noon-10.30pm Mon-Sat, 12.30-10.30pm Sun; 📶🖊🚻; 🚲16, 22, 35, 36)

Shore

SEAFOOD ££

6 🍴 Map p108, C3

The atmospheric dining room in the popular Shore pub is a haven of wood-panelled peace, with old photographs, nautical knick-knacks, fresh flowers and an open fire adding to the romantic theme. The menu changes regularly and specialises in fresh Scottish seafood, beef, pork and game. (📞0131-553 5080; www.fishersrestaurants.co.uk; 3-4 The Shore; mains £12-26;

⊙noon-10.30pm Mon-Sat, 12.30-10.30pm Sun; 📶🚻; 🚲16, 22, 35, 36)

A Room in Leith

SCOTTISH ££

7 🍴 Map p108, C2

This restaurant (and its companion bar, Teuchters Landing (p111)) inhabits a warren of nooks and crannies in a red-brick building (once a waiting room for ferries across the Firth of Forth), with a bright conservatory and outdoor tables on a floating terrace in the dock. The Scottish-flavoured menu includes haggis with Arran mustard-and-thyme cream sauce, and braised lamb with port gravy. (📞0131-554 7427; www.aroomin.co.uk; 1c Dock Pl; 2-/3-course dinner £20/25; ⊙noon-3pm Fri-Sun, 5-9.45pm daily; 📶🚻; 🚲16, 22, 35, 36)

Local Life
Cramond Village

Originally a mill village, Cramond has a historic 17th-century church and a 15th-century tower house, as well as some rather unimpressive Roman remains, but most people come to enjoy the walks along the river to the ruined mills and to stroll along the seafront. On the riverside, opposite the cottage on the far bank, is the Maltings, which hosts an interesting exhibition on Cramond's history. With its moored yachts, stately swans and whitewashed houses spilling down the hillside at the mouth of the River Almond, Cramond is the most picturesque corner of Edinburgh.

Drinking

Roseleaf

BAR

8 🍺 Map p108, B3

Cute, quaint and verging on chintzy, the Roseleaf could hardly be further from the average Leith bar. Decked out in flowered wallpaper, old furniture and rose-patterned china (cocktails are served in teapots), the real ales and bottled beers are complemented by a range of speciality teas, coffees and fruit drinks (including rose lemonade), and well-above-average pub grub (served from 10am to 10pm). (📞0131-476 5268; www.roseleaf.co.uk; 23-24 Sandport Pl; ⊙10am-1am; 📶🚻; 🚲16, 22, 35, 36)

Lioness of Leith

BAR

9 📍 Map p108, C5

Duke St was always one of the rougher corners of Leith, but the emergence of pubs like the Lioness is a sure sign of creeping gentrification. Distressed timber and battered leather benches are surrounded by vintage *objets trouvés* from chandeliers and glitterballs to mounted animal heads, a pinball machine and a pop-art print of Allen Ginsberg. Good beers and cocktails. (📞0131-629 0580; www. facebook.com/Thelionessofleith; 21-25 Duke St; ⏰noon-midnight Mon-Thu, 11am-1am Fri & Sat, 12.30pm-midnight Sun; 📶; 🚌21, 25, 34, 35, 49)

Teuchters Landing

PUB

A cosy warren of timber-lined nooks and crannies housed in a single-storey red-brick building (once a waiting room for ferries across the Firth of Forth), this real-ale and malt-whisky bar (see 7 ✖ Map p108, C2) also has outdoor tables on a floating terrace in the dock. (📞0131-554 7427; www.aroomin.co.uk; 1 Dock Pl; ⏰10.30am-1am; 📶; 🚌16, 22, 35, 36)

Old Chain Pier

PUB

10 📍 Map p108, A2

The delightful Old Chain Pier enjoys a brilliant location overlooking the sea. The building was once the 19th-century booking office for steamers crossing the Firth of Forth (the pier from which it takes its name was washed away in a storm in 1898).

The bar serves real ales, bottled craft beers, cocktails and wines, and the kitchen serves excellent pub grub. (📞0131-552 4960; http://oldchainpier.com; 32 Trinity Cres; ⏰11.30am-11pm Sun-Thu, to 1am Fri & Sat; 📶; 🚌16)

Shopping

Ocean Terminal

MALL

11 🔒 Map p108, A1

Anchored by Debenhams and BHS department stores, Ocean Terminal is the biggest shopping centre in Edinburgh; fashion outlets include Fat Face, GAP, Schuh, Superdry and White Stuff. The complex also includes access to the former Royal Yacht *Britannia* and a berth for visiting cruise liners. (📞0131-555 8888; www.oceanterminal.com; Ocean Dr; ⏰10am-8pm Mon-Fri, to 7pm Sat, 11am-6pm Sun; 📶; 🚌11, 22, 34, 35, 36)

Kinloch Anderson

FASHION & ACCESSORIES

12 🔒 Map p108, B3

One of the best tartan shops in Edinburgh, Kinloch Anderson was founded in 1868 and is still family run. It is a supplier of kilts and Highland dress to the royal family. (📞0131-555 1390; www.kinlochanderson. com; 4 Dock St; ⏰9am-5.30pm Mon-Sat; 🚌16, 22, 35, 36)

Explore

South Edinburgh

Stretching south from the Old Town and taking in the 19th-century tenements of Tollcross, Bruntsfield and Marchmont, and the upmarket suburbs of Newington, Grange and Morningside, this is a peaceful residential neighbourhood of smart Victorian flats and spacious garden villas. There's not much to see in the way of tourist attractions, but there are many good restaurants, cafes and pubs.

The Sights in a Day

☀️ Start the day with breakfast at **Peter's Yard** (p118), then enjoy a leisurely stroll through the **Meadows** (p116) – look to see if there's a cricket match in progress. Spend the rest of the morning browsing the exhibits at the **Surgeons' Hall Museums** (pictured left; p116) before sitting down to a lunch of Indian 'tapas' at **Mother India's Cafe** (p118).

☀️ In the afternoon, take a bus to **Blackford Hill** (p116), and spend an hour or two exploring the walking trails here and in the neighbouring **Hermitage of Braid** (p116). Climb to the summit of the hill for a glorious late-afternoon view across the city to the castle, the Old Town skyline and Arthur's Seat.

🌙 Book well in advance to be sure of a table at **Aizle** (p116), and check the listings to see if there's a show on at the **Festival Theatre** (p120). If it's a sunny summer evening you might prefer to indulge in outdoor drinks at **Pear Tree House** (p120).

❤️ Best of Edinburgh

Drinking
Bennet's Bar (p119)

Auld Hoose (p119)

Brauhaus (p119)

Eating
Aizle (p116)

First Coast (p117)

Locanda de Gusti (p117)

Shopping
Word Power (p121)

Museums & Galleries
Surgeons' Hall Museums (p116)

Getting There

🚌 **Bus** The main bus routes south from the city centre are 10, 11, 15, 16, 17, 23, 27 and 45 from the west end of Princes St to Tollcross (all except 10 and 27 continue south to Bruntsfield and Morningside); and 3, 5, 7, 8, 29, 31, 37, 47 and 49 from North Bridge to Newington.

A   **B**   West End   **C**   **D**   Edinburgh Castle

WEST END
W Maitland St
Canning St
Lothian Rd
Spittal St
W Port

Haymarket
Morrison St
Morrison St   Bread St

Haymarket Station
Dalry Rd
Dalry Pl

7
6
Orwell Pl
Caledonian Cres
W Approach Rd

Gardner's Cres

Earl Grey St
Lauriston Gdns

FOUNTAIN-BRIDGE
Fountainbridge
Ponton St
TOLLCROSS
14

Fountainpark Leisure Centre
Gilmore Park
Lochrin Pl
Biketrax
18
Brougham Pl

Union Canal
Gilmore Pl
Leven St
12
Glengyle Tce

Dundee St
Gillespie Cres
11
Bruntsfield Links

Learmington Tce
Morningside Rd
Whitehouse Loan
Warrender Park Tce

Polwarth Cres
Granville Tce
Viewforth
MERCHISTON
Warrender Park Rd

Polwarth Gdns
Montpelier Park
Merchiston Ave
Merchiston Park
Merchiston Pl
Forbes Rd
Greenhill Gdns
Greenhill Rd
Greenhill Tce

Polwarth Tce
E Castle Rd
W Castle Rd
Merchiston Cres

Napier Rd
Napier University
Chamberlain Rd
GREENHILL
Strathearn Pl

N   0 ___ 400 m
    0 ___ 0.2 miles

2
4

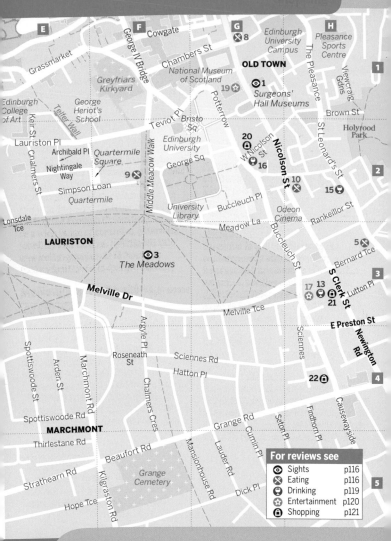

E
Grassmarket

F
Cowgate
George IV Bridge
Chambers St
Greyfriars
Kirkyard
National Museum
of Scotland

G
⊗8
Edinburgh
University
Campus
The Pleasance

H
Pleasance
Sports
Centre
Viewcraig
Gdns

1

OLD TOWN

Edinburgh
College
of Art

George
Heriot's
School
Telfer Wall

19 ☆

⊙1
Surgeons'
Hall Museums

Brown St

Holyrood
Park

Keir St
Chalmers St

Lauriston Pl
Archibald Pl
Nightingale
Way
9 ⊗

Teviot Pl
Bristo
Sq
Edinburgh
University
George Sq

Quartermile
Square

Simpson Loan
Quartermile

20
🔒
W Nicolson
St
19 🔒
16

Nicolson St

St Leonard's St

2

Lonsdale
Tce

University
Library

Buccleuch Pl

10
⊗

Odeon
Cinema

Rankeillor St

15 ☆

LAURISTON

⊙3
The Meadows

Middle Meadow Walk

Meadow La

Buccleuch St

5 ⊗
Bernard Tce
3

Melville Dr

Melville Tce

17 13
☆   ☆
21

S Clerk St Lutton Pl

E Preston St
Newington
Rd

Argyle Pl
Roseneath
St

Sciennes Rd
Hatton Pl

Sciennes

22 🔒

4

Spottiswoode St
Arden St
Marchmont Rd

Chalmers Cres

Grange Rd

Seton Pl
Findhorn Pl

Causewayside

Spottiswoode Rd

MARCHMONT
Thirlestane Rd

Beaufort Rd

Lauder Rd

Cumin Pl

Mansionhouse Rd

Stratheam Rd
Hope Tce
Kilgraston Rd

Grange
Cemetery

Dick Pl

For reviews see
⊙ Sights   p116
⊗ Eating   p116
⊗ Drinking   p119
☆ Entertainment   p120
🔒 Shopping   p121

5

Sights

Surgeons' Hall Museums
MUSEUM

1 ◉ Map p114, G1

Housed in a grand Ionic temple designed by William Playfair in 1832, these three fascinating museums were originally established as teaching collections. The **History of Surgery Museum** provides a look at surgery in Scotland from the 15th century – when barbers supplemented their income with bloodletting, amputations and other surgical procedures – to the present day. The highlight is the exhibit on **Burke and Hare**, which includes Burke's death mask and a pocketbook made from his skin. (www.museum. rcsed.ac.uk; Nicolson St; adult/child £6/3.50; ☺10am-5pm daily Apr-Oct, noon-4pm Mon-Fri Nov-Mar; ☐all South Bridge buses)

Hermitage of Braid
WILDLIFE RESERVE

2 ◉ Map p114, C5

The Hermitage of Braid is a wooded valley criss-crossed with walking trails to the south of Blackford Hill – with sunlight filtering through the leaves and the sound of birdsong all around, you'll feel miles from the city here. **Hermitage House** (Hermitage of Braid; ☺9am-4pm Mon-Fri, noon-4pm Sun, closed Sat; ☐5, 11, 15, 16), an 18th-century mansion, houses a visitor centre that explains the history and wildlife of the glen, and has details of nearby nature trails. (www.fohb. org; ☐5, 11, 15, 16)

The Meadows
PARK

3 ◉ Map p114, F3

This mile-long stretch of lush grass (pictured right) criss-crossed with tree-lined walks was once a shallow lake known as the Borough Loch. Drained in the 1740s and converted into parkland, it's a great place for a picnic or a quiet stroll – in springtime its walks lie ankle-deep in drifts of pink cherry blossom, and there are great views of Arthur's Seat. (Melville Dr; ☐all Tollcross, South Bridge buses)

Blackford Hill
VIEWPOINT

4 ◉ Map p114, D5

A patch of countryside enclosed by the city's southern suburbs, craggy Blackford Hill (164m) offers pleasant walking and splendid views. The panorama to the north takes in Edinburgh Castle atop its rock, the bristling spine of the Old Town, the monuments on Calton Hill and the 'sleeping lion' of Arthur's Seat. (Charterhall Rd; ☐24, 38, 41)

Eating

Aizle
SCOTTISH $$

5 ✕ Map p114, H3

If you're the sort who has trouble deciding what to eat, Aizle will do it for you (the name is an old Scots word for 'spark' or 'ember'). There's no menu, just a five-course dinner conjured from a monthly 'harvest' of the finest and

The Meadows

freshest of local produce (listed on a blackboard), and presented beautifully – art on a plate. (📞0131-662 9349; http://aizle.co.uk; 107-109 St Leonard's St; 5-course dinner £45; ⏰6-9.30pm Wed, Thu & Sun, 5-9.30pm Fri & Sat; 🛜; 🚌14)

First Coast
SCOTTISH $$

6 🍴 Map p114, A2

This popular neighbourhood bistro has a striking main dining area with sea-blue wood panelling and stripped stonework, and a short and simple menu offering hearty comfort food such as fish with creamy mash, brown shrimp and garlic butter, or leek and bread pudding, creamed leeks and braised fennel. Lunchtime and early

evening there's an excellent two-course meal for £12.50. (📞0131-313 4404; www.first-coast.co.uk; 97-101 Dalry Rd; mains £12-20; ⏰noon-2pm & 5-11pm Mon-Sat; 🛜✏️👶; 🚌2, 3, 4, 25, 33, 44)

Locanda de Gusti
ITALIAN $$

7 🍴 Map p114, A2

This bustling family bistro, loud with the buzz of conversation and the clink of glasses and cutlery, is no ordinary Italian but a little corner of Naples complete with hearty Neapolitan home cooking by friendly head chef Rosario. The food ranges from light and tasty ravioli tossed with butter and sage to delicious platters of grilled seafood. (📞0131-346

8800; www.locandadegusti.com; 102 Dalry Rd; mains £9-26; ⏱5.30-10pm Mon-Sat, 12.30-2.15pm Thu-Sat; 🍴; 🚌2, 3, 4, 25, 33, 44)

Mother India's Cafe INDIAN $$

8 ✖️ Map p114, G1

A simple concept pioneered in Glasgow has captured hearts and minds – and stomachs – here in Edinburgh: Indian food served in tapas-size portions, so that you can sample a greater variety of deliciously different dishes without busting a gut. Hugely popular, so book a table to avoid disappointment. (📞0131-524 9801; www.motherindia.co.uk; 3-5 Infirmary St; dishes £4-6; ⏱noon-2pm & 5-10.30pm Mon-Wed, noon-11pm Thu-Sun; 📶🍴; 🚌all South Bridge buses)

🅠 Local Life
Southside Brunch

One of South Edinburgh's favourite places to kick back over brunch with the weekend papers, **Loudon's** (Map p114, C2; www.loudons-cafe.co.uk; 94b Fountainbridge; mains £5-10; ⏱8am-5pm; 📶📵🍴; 🚌1, 34, 35) is a cafe that bakes its own organic bread, serves ethically sourced coffee, and has a weekend brunch menu (8am to 3pm Saturday and Sunday) that includes eggs Benedict, warm spiced quinoa with dried fruit, and specials such as blueberry pancakes with fruit salad.

Peter's Yard CAFE $

9 ✖️ Map p114, F2

This Swedish-style coffee house produces its own home-baked breads, from sourdough to focaccia, which form the basis of lunchtime sandwiches with fillings such as roast beef with beetroot and caper salad, and roast butternut squash with sunblush tomato pesto. Breakfast (served till noon) can be a basket of breads with conserves and cheeses, or yoghurt with granola and fruit. (📞0131-228 5876; www.petersyard.com; 27 Simpson Loan; mains £5-9; ⏱7.30am-6pm Mon-Fri, 9am-6pm Sat & Sun; 📵🍴; 🚌23, 27, 35, 45, 47)

Kalpna INDIAN $

10 ✖️ Map p114, H2

A long-standing Edinburgh favourite, Kalpna is one of the best Indian restaurants in the country, vegetarian or otherwise. The cuisine is mostly Gujarati, with a smattering of dishes from other parts of India. The all-you-can-eat lunch buffet (£8) is superb value. (📞0131-667 9890; www.kalpnarestaurant.com; 2-3 St Patrick Sq; mains £6-11; ⏱noon-2pm & 5.30-9.30pm Mon-Sat year-round, 6pm-10.30pm Sun May-Sep; 📵; 🚌all Newington buses)

Katie's Diner AMERICAN $$

11 ✖️ Map p114, D3

As you might expect from a place run by a husband-and-wife team, this cute little diner has a warm welcome and a homey atmosphere. The handful of tables enjoy a view onto the parkland of Bruntsfield Links, and the menu ranges from barbecue chicken wings and panko prawns to prime Scottish steaks and juicy home-made burgers. (☑0131-229 1394; www.katiesdiner.com; 12 Barclay Tce; mains £9-24; ☺6-9pm Tue-Thu, to 9.30pm Fri & Sat; ☐all Bruntsfield buses)

Drinking

Bennet's Bar

PUB

12 🍷 Map p114, D3

Situated beside the King's Theatre, Bennet's has managed to hang on to almost all of its beautiful Victorian fittings, from the leaded stained-glass windows and ornate mirrors to the wooden gantry and the brass water taps on the bar (for your whisky – there are over 100 malts from which to choose). (☑0131-229 5143; www.bennetsbaredinburgh.co.uk; 8 Leven St; ☺11am-1am; ☐all Tollcross buses)

Royal Dick

MICROBREWERY

13 🍷 Map p114, H3

The quirky decor at the Royal Dick alludes to its past as the home of Edinburgh University's veterinary school: there are shelves of laboratory glassware, walls covered with animal bones, even an old operating table. But rather than being creepy, it's a warm and welcoming place for a drink, serving craft gins, malt whiskies, and ales produced by its own

microbrewery. (☑0131-560 1572; www.summerhall.co.uk/the-royal-dick; 1 Summerhall; ☺noon-1am Mon-Sat, 12.30pm-midnight Sun; 🛜; ☐41, 42, 67)

Brauhaus

BAR

14 🍷 Map p114, D2

This bar is fairly small – half a dozen bar stools, a couple of sofas and a scattering of seats – but its ambition is huge, with a vast menu of bottled beers from all over the world, ranging from the usual suspects (Belgium, Germany and the Czech Republic), to more unusual brews such as Paradox Smokehead (a 10% ABV stout aged for six months in a whisky cask). (☑0131-447 7721; 105 Lauriston Pl; ☺5pm-1am Sun-Fri, 3pm-1am Sat; ☐23, 27, 35, 45)

Auld Hoose

PUB

15 🍷 Map p114, H2

Promoting itself as the Southside's only 'alternative' pub, the Auld Hoose certainly lives up to its reputation, with unpretentious decor, gig posters on the walls, a range of real ales from remote Scottish microbreweries (Trashy Blonde from Brewdog on Arran, Avalanche Ale from Loch Fyne in Argyll), and a jukebox that would make the late John Peel weep with joy. (☑0131-668 2934; www.theauldhoose.co.uk; 23-25 St Leonards St; ☺noon-12.45am Mon-Sat, 12.30pm-12.45am Sun; 🛜; ☐14)

Local Life

Union Canal

Built 200 years ago and abandoned in the 1960s, the Union Canal was restored and reopened to navigation in 2002. Edinburgh Quays, its city-centre terminus in Tollcross, is a starting point for canal cruises, towpath walks and bike rides. The canal stretches west for 31 miles through the rural landscape of West Lothian to Falkirk, where it joins the Forth and Clyde Canal at the Falkirk Wheel boat lift. At Harrison Park, a mile southwest of Edinburgh Quays, is a pretty little canal basin with rowing boats for hire.

Pear Tree House   PUB

16 ⭑ Map p114, G2

Set in an 18th-century house with a cobbled courtyard, the Pear Tree is a student favourite with an open fire in winter, comfy sofas and board games inside, plus the city's biggest and most popular beer garden in summer. (☑0131-667 7533; www.pear-tree-house.co.uk; 38 West Nicolson St; ⊙11am-1am; 🛜; 🚌2, 41, 42, 47)

Entertainment

Summerhall   THEATRE

17 ⭑ Map p114, H3

Formerly Edinburgh University's veterinary school, the Summerhall complex is a major cultural centre and entertainment venue, with old halls and lecture theatres (including an original anatomy lecture theatre) now serving as venues for drama, dance, cinema and comedy performances. It's also one of the main venues for Edinburgh Festival events. (☑0131-560 1580; www.summerhall.co.uk; 1 Summerhall; 🚌41, 42, 67)

Cameo   CINEMA

18 ⭑ Map p114, D2

The three-screen, independently owned Cameo is a good, old-fashioned cinema showing an imaginative mix of mainstream and art-house movies. There is a good program of late-night films and Sunday matinees, and the seats in screen 1 are big enough to get lost in. (☑0871 902 5723; www.picturehouses.co.uk; 38 Home St; 🛜; 🚌all Tollcross buses)

Edinburgh Festival Theatre   THEATRE

19 ⭑ Map p114, G1

A beautifully restored art-deco theatre with a modern frontage, the Festival is the city's main venue for opera, dance and ballet, but also stages musicals, concerts, drama and children's shows. (☑0131-529 6000; www.edtheatres.com/festival; 13-29 Nicolson St; ⊙box office 10am-6pm Mon-Sat, to 8pm show nights, 4pm-showtime Sun; 🚌all South Bridge buses)

LONELY PLANET/GETTY IMAGES ©

Bennet's Bar (p119)

Shopping

Word Power
BOOKS

20 🔒 Map p114, G2

A radical, independent bookshop that supports both small publishers and local writers. It stocks a wide range of political, gay and feminist literature, as well as non-mainstream fiction and nonfiction. (📞0131-662 9112; www.word-power.co.uk; 43 West Nicolson St; ⏱10am-6pm Mon-Sat, noon-5pm Sun; 🚍41, 42)

Hogs Head Music
MUSIC

21 🔒 Map p114, H3

A classic old-school music and film shop that buys and sells second-hand CDs and DVDs. Thousands of disks and box sets to browse through, a range of T-shirts, and staff who really know their stuff. (📞0131-667 5274; www.hogs-head.com; 62 South Clerk St; ⏱10am-5.30pm Mon-Sat, 12.30-4.30pm Sun; 🚍all Newington buses)

Courtyard Antiques
ANTIQUES

22 🔒 Map p114, H4

Hidden down a lane, the Courtyard has two crowded floors of wooden furniture (19th century to the 1970s), toys and militaria, including some fascinating bric-a-brac that ranges from 78rpm records to model trains, boats and aircraft. (📞0131-662 9008; www.edinburgh-courtyardantiques.co.uk; 108a Causewayside; ⏱9.30am-5.30pm; 🚍42)

Top Sights
Rosslyn Chapel

Getting There

🚌 **Bus** Lothian Bus 37 runs from the west end of Princes St in Edinburgh to the village of Roslin (£1.60, 45 minutes, every 30 minutes).

The success of Dan Brown's novel *The Da Vinci Code* and the subsequent Hollywood film has seen a flood of visitors descend on Scotland's most beautiful and enigmatic church (which features in the novel's finale).

Rosslyn Chapel was built in the mid-15th century for William St Clair, third earl of Orkney, and the ornately carved interior – at odds with the architectural fashion of its time – is a monument to the mason's art, rich in symbolic imagery and shrouded in mystery.

The Apprentice Pillar

Perhaps the most beautiful of its carvings, the Apprentice Pillar is at the entrance to the Lady Chapel. Four vines spiral around the pillar, issuing from the mouths of eight dragons at its base. At the top is an image of Isaac, son of Abraham, upon the altar.

Lucifer, the Fallen Angel

To the left of the second window from the left in the Lady Chapel is an upside-down angel bound with rope, a symbol associated with Freemasonry. The *Dance of Death* decorates the arch above.

The Green Man

In the Lady Chapel, on the boss at the base of the arch between the second and third windows from the left, is the *Green Man*. It's the finest example of more than 100 carvings of the 'green man', a pagan symbol of spring, fertility and rebirth.

Indian Corn

The frieze around the second window in the south wall is said to represent Indian corn (maize), but predates Columbus' discovery of the New World in 1492. Other carvings resemble aloe vera, also American in origin.

The Apprentice

High in the southwest corner is the head of the murdered apprentice; there's a deep wound in his forehead, above the right eye. Legend says the stonemason's apprentice created a pillar more exquisitely carved than anything the mason himself could achieve and, in a fit of jealousy, the mason murdered him. The head on the side wall to the left is the apprentice's mother.

The Ceiling

The spectacular ceiling vault is decorated with engraved roses, lilies and stars; can you spot the sun and the moon?

Collegiate Church of St Matthew

www.rosslynchapel.org.uk

Chapel Loan, Roslin ; **P**

adult/child £9/free

⊙9.30am-6pm Mon-Sat Apr-Sep, to 5.30pm Oct-Mar, noon-4.45pm Sun year-round

---

☑ Top Tips

▶ Get your tickets in advance through the chapel's website (except in August, when no bookings are taken).

▶ No photography is allowed inside the chapel.

▶ Buy the official guidebook, find a bench in the gardens and have a skim through before going into the chapel – the background information will make your visit all the more interesting.

✗ Take a Break

There's a **coffee shop** (mains £5-6; ⊙10am-5pm Mon-Sat, noon-4pm Sun) in the chapel's visitor centre, serving soup, sandwiches, coffee and cake, with a view over Roslin Glen.

The Best of

Edinburgh

Edinburgh's Best Walks

Edinburgh's Best...

Scottish National Gallery (p74)
PAUL RAEBURN/NATIONAL GALLERIES OF SCOTLAND ©

Best Walks
From Castle to Palace

🏃 The Walk

Edinburgh Castle, the Palace of Holyroodhouse and the Scottish Parliament are what make Edinburgh Scotland's capital. This walk links the city's most iconic sights by following (mostly) the Royal Mile, the ancient processional route followed by kings and queens travelling between castle and palace. Our route occasionally shifts sideways to explore the narrow closes and wynds that lend Edinburgh's Old Town its unique, historic atmosphere.

Start Edinburgh Castle

Finish Palace of Holyroodhouse

Length 1.5 miles; one hour

✗ Take a Break

Victoria St and the Grassmarket, a few minutes' walk south of the Royal Mile, are crammed with places to eat, while **Devil's Advocate** (p45) lies down a close on the north side. Further down the Royal Mile, **Wedgwood** (p43) offers fine dining Scottish style.

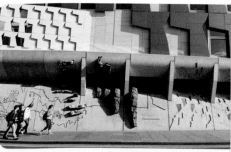

LONELY PLANET/GETTY IMAGES ©

Scottish Parliament Building (p56)

❶ Edinburgh Castle

Dominating the city from its superb defensive position, **Edinburgh Castle** (p24) is one of Britain's most impressive fortresses. Check out the Scottish Crown Jewels, wander through the former prisons in the Castle Vaults, and try not to jump when the One O'Clock Gun is fired.

❷ Scotch Whisky Experience

After enjoying the views from the **Castle Esplanade**, head down the Royal Mile. On the left you'll pass the **Witches Well** (a fountain commemorating those executed on suspicion of witchcraft) before reaching the **Scotch Whisky Experience** (p38)

❸ Writers' Museum

Descend Ramsay Lane to the twin towers of Edinburgh's **New College**, and see the **statue of John Knox** in the courtyard. Return to the Royal Mile via **Lady Stair's Close**, a picturesque Old Town alley, and the **Writers' Museum** (p40)

❹ St Giles Cathedral

Continue down the High St to **St Giles Cathedral** (p38), Edinburgh's most important church. Follow Parliament Sq around the south side of the church, and take a look at **Parliament Hall** and the **Mercat Cross**.

❺ Real Mary King's Close

Back on the High St is the Georgian facade of the **city chambers** (seat of Edinburgh city council), which was built over a medieval Old Town

alley with eerie remains you can explore on a tour of the **Real Mary King's Close** (p28).

❻ Museum of Edinburgh

Descend **Advocate's Close**, one of the most atmospheric of the Old Town's wynds, then climb back to the Royal Mile along **Cockburn St**, lined with trendy boutiques. Continue down the High St, past **John Knox House** (p40), to the **Museum of Edinburgh** (p38)

❼ Scottish Parliament Building

Opposite **Canongate Kirk**, go down Crighton's Close past the **Scottish Poetry Library**, then left and left again up Reid's Close, to see the **Scottish Parliament Building** (p56).

❽ Palace of Holyroodhouse

The Royal Mile ends at the ornate gates of the **Palace of Holyroodhouse** (p54), the official residence of the royal family when they're in town.

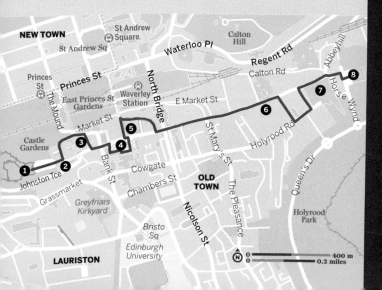

![Walking figure icon] **Best Walks**
Charlotte Square to Calton Hill

🏃 The Walk

Edinburgh's New Town is one of the world's finest Georgian cityscapes, well worthy of its Unesco World Heritage status. This walk captures the essence of the New Town's Georgian elegance, taking in its two architecturally pivotal squares, the grand town houses of Heriot Row (complete with private gardens), and two of the city's best viewpoints, the Scott Monument and Calton Hill.

Start Charlotte Sq

Finish Calton Hill

Length 1.5 miles; one hour

🍴 Take a Break

Thistle St is home to a good selection of bistros and restaurants – try **Café Marlayne** (☎0131-226 2230; www.cafemarlayne.com; 76 Thistle St; mains lunch £8-10, dinner £15-18; ☻noon-10pm; 🚌24, 29, 42) for some French home cooking, or **Fishers in the City** (p80) for a seafood feast.

Charlotte Square

❶ Charlotte Square

Charlotte Square (p75) is a masterpiece of neoclassical design. On the north side is the museum **Georgian House** (p75), while off the southeast corner is **16 South Charlotte St**, birthplace of telephone pioneer Alexander Graham Bell.

❷ Oxford Bar

Leave the square at its northeast corner and turn right along Young St, passing the **Oxford Bar** (p81), made famous by Ian Rankin's Inspector Rebus novels. Turn left on N Castle St, right on Queen St then left again, taking a peek into the private **Queen Street Gardens**.

❸ Heriot Row

Turn right into Heriot Row, a typically elegant New Town terrace. At No 17, an inscription marks the house where writer Robert Louis Stevenson spent his childhood. It's said that the island in the pond in Queen Street Gardens (not open to the public) was the inspiration for *Treasure Island*.

4 George Street

Go uphill to George St and turn left. This was once the centre of Edinburgh's financial industry; now the banks and offices have been taken over by designer boutiques and cocktail bars. Pop into the **Dome Grill Room** at No 14, formerly a bank, to see the ornate Georgian banking hall.

5 St Andrew Square

The New Town's most impressive square is dominated by the **Melville Monument**, commemorating Henry Dundas (1742–1811), the most powerful Scottish politician of his time. On the far side is **Dundas House**, a Palladian mansion that houses the head office of the Royal Bank of Scotland (another magnificent domed banking hall lies within).

6 Scott Monument

South St David St leads past **Jenners** (p70), the grand dame of Edinburgh department stores, to the **Scott Monument** (p69). Climb the 287 steps to the top for an incomparable view over **Princes Street Gardens** (p68) to the castle.

7 Calton Hill

Head east along Princes St and Waterloo Pl to the stairs on the left, just after the side street called Calton Hill. Climb to the summit of **Calton Hill** (p76), one of Edinburgh's finest viewpoints, with a panorama that stretches from the Firth of Forth to the Pentland Hills.

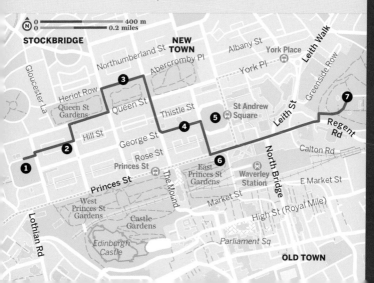

Best Eating

Eating out in Edinburgh has changed beyond all recognition in the last 20 years. Two decades ago, sophisticated dining meant a visit to the Aberdeen Angus Steak House for a prawn cocktail, steak (well done) and chips, and Black Forest gateau. Today, eating out has become a commonplace event and the city has more restaurants per head of population than any other city in the UK, including a handful of Michelin stars.

Modern Scottish Cuisine

Scotland has never been celebrated for its national cuisine – in fact, from haggis and porridge to deep-fried Mars Bars, it has more often been an object of ridicule. But a new culinary style known as Modern Scottish has emerged, where chefs take top-quality Scottish produce – from Highland venison, Aberdeen Angus beef and freshly landed seafood to root vegetables, raspberries and Ayrshire cheeses – and prepare it simply, in a way that enhances the natural flavours, often adding a French, Italian or Asian twist.

Haggis – Scotland's National Dish

The raw ingredients of Scotland's national dish don't sound too promising – the finely chopped lungs, heart and liver of a sheep, mixed with oatmeal and onion and stuffed into a sheep's stomach bag. However, it actually tastes surprisingly good and is now on the menu in many of the capital's restaurants, whether served with the traditional accompaniment of *champit tatties* (mashed potatoes) and *bashed neeps* (turnips) with a generous dollop of butter and a good sprinkling of black pepper, or given a modern twist (such as haggis in filo pastry parcels with hoisin sauce).

LONELY PLANET/GETTY IMAGES ©

☑ Top Tips

▶ Book well in advance (at least a month ahead for August) to be sure of a table at top restaurants.

▶ The Edinburgh & Glasgow Eating & Drinking Guide (www.list.co.uk/ead) contains reviews of around 800 restaurants, cafes and bars.

▶ The www.5pm. co.uk website lists last-minute offers from restaurants with tables to spare that evening.

Best Modern Scottish

Martin Wishart Edinburgh's first Michelin star still shines brightly, adding French flair to Scottish ingredients. (p109)

Timberyard Slow-food restaurant with emphasis on locally sourced produce. (p90)

Castle Terrace Seasonal menu makes the best of fine Scottish produce. (p90)

Wedgwood Foraged salad leaves add originality to informal fine dining. (p43)

Aizle The finest and freshest of local produce, gorgeously presented. (p116)

Kitchin Michelin-starred excellence from TV chef Tom Kitchin. (p109)

Best Traditional Scottish

Tower Specialities include Scottish oysters and Aberdeen Angus steaks, with a great view of the castle. (p44)

Scottish Cafe & Restaurant Traditional dishes such as Cullen skink (smoked haddock soup) and haggis served in the National Gallery complex. (p69)

Amber Set in the Scotch Whisky Experience; many dishes include whisky in the recipe. (p44)

McKirdy's Steakhouse Prime Scottish beef, simply prepared and served in friendly informal setting. (p91)

Witchery by the Castle Wonderfully over-the-top Gothic decor, great steak and seafood, and fine wines. (p43)

Cannonball Restaurant Fine Scottish dining right next door to Edinburgh Castle. (p43)

Best Informal Dining

Gardener's Cottage Set menu of homegrown vegetables, foraged mushrooms and sustainable fish served at communal tables. (p77)

First Coast Great neighbourhood bistro with satisfying menu of Scottish and international favourites. (p117)

Dogs Good-value bistro makes the most of cheaper cuts of meat; beef cheeks, oxtail, liver and onions. (p77)

Café Marlayne Cosy, farmhouse-kitchen atmosphere and tasty French home cooking. (p128)

Mums Retro cafe serving old-fashioned comfort food, like sausages, mash and onion gravy. (p43)

Locanda de Gusti A little corner of Naples complete with hearty Neapolitan home cooking. (p117)

Best Seafood

Ondine Arguably the best seafood restaurant in town, with low-lit romantic atmosphere. (p42)

Fishers Bistro Always busy and bustling, everything from humble fishcakes to the finest oysters. (p109)

Shore Pleasantly informal restaurant with Leith waterfront setting, serves game as well as seafood. (p110)

Best Vegetarian

David Bann Smart and sophisticated, brings an inventive approach to vegetarian food. (p43)

Kalpna Long-established Indian restaurant, famous for its all-you-can-eat lunch buffet. (p118)

Best
Drinking

Edinburgh has always been a drinker's city. It has more than 700 pubs – more per square mile than any other UK city – and they are as varied and full of character as the people who drink in them, from Victorian palaces to stylish pre-club bars, and from real-ale howffs to trendy cocktail lounges.

WILL ROBB/GETTY IMAGES ©

Trad vs Trendy

At one end of Edinburgh's broad spectrum of hostelries lies the traditional 19th-century bar, which has preserved much of its original Victorian decoration and generally serves cask-conditioned real ales and a staggering range of malt whiskies. At the other end is the modern cocktail bar, with a cool clientele and styling so sharp you could cut yourself on it.

Edinburgh Beers

In the 19th century, Edinburgh ranked alongside Munich, Pilsen and Burton-on-Trent in importance as a brewing centre, boasting 28 breweries. in the early 1900s. Today the city's two large-scale breweries – Caledonian (now part-owned by Scottish Newcastle), creator of Deuchars IPA (available in most of the city's real-ale pubs); and Stewart Brewing, producer of Edinburgh Gold – have been joined by an ever-growing number of microbreweries.

Opening Times

Pubs generally open from 11am to 11pm Monday to Saturday and 12.30pm to 11pm on Sunday. Many open later on Friday and Saturday, and close at midnight or 1am, while those with a food or music licence can party on until 3am. The bell for last orders rings about 15 minutes before closing time, with 15 minutes' drinking-up time after the bar closes.

☑ **Top Tips**

▶ The Gig Guide (www.gigguide. co.uk) is a free monthly email newsletter and listings website covering live music in Edinburgh pubs.

▶ If you want to avoid the crowds on Friday and Saturday nights, steer clear of the Grassmarket, the Cowgate and Lothian Rd.

Café Royal Circle Bar (p80)

Best Historic Pubs

Bennet's Bar Locals' pub with lovely Victorian fittings, from stained glass to brass water taps on the bar. (p119)

Café Royal Circle Bar City-centre haven of Victorian splendour, famed for Doulton ceramic portraits. (p80)

Sheep Heid Inn Semirural retreat in the shadow of Arthur's Seat, famed as Edinburgh's oldest pub. (p63)

Guildford Arms A time capsule of polished mahogany and gleaming brass. (p81)

Best Real-Ale Pubs

Holyrood 9A Modern take on traditional pub, with no fewer than 20 beers on tap. (p46)

Blue Blazer Resolutely old-fashioned pub with good range of Scottish ales. (p92)

Stockbridge Tap More lounge bar than pub, but with seven real ales on offer. (p102)

BrewDog Lively, modern bar owned by one of Scotland's most innovative microbreweries. (p47)

Auld Hoose Great jukebox plus broad range of beers from Scottish microbreweries. (p119)

Best Cocktail Bars

Bramble Possibly the city's best cocktails, served in an atmospheric cellar bar. (p81)

Tigerlily Cocktails as colourful as the swirling, glittering designer decor. (p82)

Villager Laid-back, sofa-strewn lounge serving great cocktails without the faff. (p48)

Best Whisky Bars

Bow Bar Busy Grassmarket-area pub with huge selection of malt whiskies. (p45)

Malt Shovel Old-school pub with more than 100 single malts behind the bar. (p47)

OX 184 A big, booming industrial-chic bar with more than 100 whiskies on offer. (p46)

Best
Shopping

Edinburgh's shopping experience extends far beyond the big-name department stores of Princes St, ranging from designer fashion and handmade jewellery to independent bookshops, delicatessens and farmers markets. Classic north-of-the-border buys include cashmere, Harris tweed, tartan goods, Celtic jewellery, smoked salmon and Scotch whisky.

ANDRZEJ TARNAWCZYK/SHUTTERSTOCK ©

Princes Street

Princes St is Edinburgh's trademark shopping strip, lined with all the big high-street stores from Marks & Spencer to BHS and Debenhams, with more upmarket designer shops a block north on George St, and many smaller specialist stores on Rose St and Thistle St. There are also two big city-centre shopping malls – **Princes Mall**, at the eastern end of Princes St next to the Balmoral Hotel, and the nearby **St James Centre** (currently undergoing a major redevelopment), at the top of Leith St – plus **Multrees Walk**, a designer shopping complex with a flagship Harvey Nichols store on the eastern side of St Andrew Sq.

Shopping Districts

Other central shopping streets include South Bridge, Nicolson St and Lothian Rd. For more offbeat shopping – including fashion, music, crafts, gifts and jewellery – head for the cobbled lanes of Cockburn, Victoria and St Mary's Sts, all leading off the Royal Mile in the Old Town; William St in the West End; and Raeburn Pl and St Stephen's St in Stockbridge. Ocean Terminal, in Leith, is the city's biggest shopping mall.

☑ **Top Tips**

▶ In shops displaying a 'Tax Free' sign, visitors from non-EU countries can claim back the 20% VAT (value-added tax) they have paid on purchased goods.

▶ Many city-centre shops stay open till 7pm or 8pm on Thursdays.

Jenners department store (p70)

Best Department Stores

Jenners The mother of all Edinburgh department stores, founded in 1838. (p70)

Harvey Nichols Four floors of designer labels, plus rooftop brasserie with grand views. (p71)

Best for Tartan

Kinloch Anderson Tailors and kiltmakers to HM the Queen and HRH the Duke of Edinburgh; 'nuff said. (p111)

Geoffrey (Tailor) Inc Kilts in all patterns from clan tartans to football-club colours. (p51)

Best for Jewellery

Galerie Mirages An Aladdin's cave of jewellery and gifts in both ethnic and contemporary designs. (p103)

Alchemia Original designs as well as specially-commissioned pieces. (p71)

Annie Smith Edinburgh designer famed for beautiful and delicate pieces reflecting nature's patterns. (p103)

Best for Books

Word Power Long-established radical bookshop specialising in political, gay and feminist literature. (p121)

McNaughtan's Bookshop Secondhand and antiquarian dealer, books on Scottish history, art and architecture. (p83)

Best Markets

Edinburgh Farmers Market Saturday feast of fresh Scottish produce, from smoked venison to organic free-range eggs. (p90)

Stockbridge Market Eclectic Sunday market that has become a focus for the local community. (p99)

Best Views

Edinburgh is one of Europe's most beautiful cities, draped across a series of rocky hills overlooking the sea. A glance in any souvenir shop will reveal a display of postcards that testify to the city's many viewpoints, both natural and artificial. Part of the pleasure of any visit to Edinburgh is simply soaking up the scenery, so set aside some time to explore the loftier parts of the city, camera in hand.

LONE PLANET/GETTY IMAGES ©

Best Natural Viewpoints

Arthur's Seat Sweeping panoramas from the highest point in Edinburgh. (p61)

Calton Hill Edinburgh's templed 'acropolis' affords a superb view along Princes St. (p76)

Blackford Hill This southern summit provides a grandstand view of Castle Rock and Arthur's Seat. (p116)

Best Architectural Viewpoints

Scott Monument Climb 287 steps to the top of this Gothic pinnacle, and look out over Princes Street Gardens. (p69)

Camera Obscura The outlook tower here provides an iconic view along the Royal Mile. (p42)

Castle Esplanade Commanding views north across the New Town, or south towards the Pentland Hills. (p24)

Best Restaurant Views

Tower Perched at the top of the National Museum of Scotland, with a superb view of the castle. (p44)

Maxie's Bistro Outdoor tables on Victoria Terrace look out over Victoria St to the Grassmarket. (p34)

Scottish Cafe & Restaurant The window tables here have a lovely outlook along Princes Street Gardens. (p69)

Best
For Kids

Edinburgh has a multitude of attractions for children, and most things to see and do are child-friendly. During the Edinburgh and Fringe Festivals there's lots of street theatre for kids, especially on High St and at the foot of the Mound, and in December there's a Ferris wheel, an open-air ice rink and fairground rides in Princes Street Gardens.

AAABBCCC/SHUTTERSTOCK ©

Best Sights for Kids

Edinburgh Castle Ask at the ticket office about the Children's Trail, which lets kids track down various treasures. (p24)

Edinburgh Zoo Giant pandas, interactive chimpanzee enclosure, penguins on parade... (p76)

Our Dynamic Earth Loads of great stuff, from earthquake simulators to real icebergs. (p61)

Camera Obscura Fascinating exhibits on illusions, magic tricks, electricity and holograms. (p42)

Real Mary King's Close Older children will enjoy the ghost stories and creepy atmosphere here. Children under five years not admitted. (p28)

Scott Monument Lots of narrow stairs to climb, grotesque carvings to spot and a view at the top. (p69)

Best Museums for Kids

National Museum of Scotland Lots of interactive exhibits, and trail leaflets for kids to follow and fill in. (p30)

Scottish National Gallery of Modern Art Great landscaped grounds for exploring – track down all the sculptures! (p86)

☑ **Top Tips**

▶ The Edinburgh Information Centre (p151) has lots of info on children's events, and you can find the handy guidebook *Edinburgh for Under Fives* in most bookshops.

▶ Kids under five travel for free on Edinburgh buses, and five- to 15-year-olds pay a flat fare of 80p.

♥ Best
Museums & Galleries

As Scotland's capital city, it's hardly surprising that Edinburgh is home to some of the country's most important museums and art collections. You can admire the Old Masters, from Titian to Turner, at the Scottish National Gallery, hone your knowledge of Scottish heritage at the National Museum of Scotland, or delve into the arcane delights of the city's lesser-known museums.

Special Events

Several of the city's major institutions host special events and after hours visits. The National Museum of Scotland stages Museum Late events throughout the year, with live music, lectures, behind-the-scenes tours and pop-up bars; while the National Gallery stages musical performances, educational talks and art lessons. Check website What's On links for details.

Admission & Access

National collections (eg National Museum of Scotland, Scottish National Gallery, Scottish National Portrait Gallery, Scottish National Gallery of Modern Art) and Edinburgh city-owned museums (Museum of Edinburgh, City Art Centre etc) have free admission, except for temporary exhibitions where a fee is often charged. Most private galleries are also free; while smaller museums often charge an entrance fee, typically around £5 (book online at some museums for discounted tickets). National collections are generally open from 10am to 5pm, with the Scottish National Gallery and Scottish National Portrait Gallery staying open till 7pm on Thursdays.

ANTON_IVANV//SHUTTERSTOCK ©

☑ **Top Tips**

▶ The national collections have useful 'trail' leaflets that guide you around their highlights.

▶ All major museums and galleries have good restaurants or cafes, often worth a visit in their own right.

Best Collections

National Museum of Scotland Beautiful setting for collections covering Scottish history, the natural world, art and engineering. (p30)

Scottish National Portrait Gallery Far more interesting than the name implies, especially after a recent revamp. (p66)

Scottish National Portrait Gallery (p66)

Scottish National Gallery Old masters, Scottish artists, and Canova's famous marble sculpture of the *Three Graces*. (p74)

Scottish National Gallery of Modern Art Pride of place goes to works by the Scottish Colourists, Eduardo Paolozzi and Barbara Hepworth. (p86)

Best Smaller Museums

Museum of Edinburgh The city: Stone Age to 20th century. (p38)

People's Story The life and work of ordinary Edinburgh folk from the 18th century onward. (p40)

Surgeons' Hall Museums Grisly but fascinating collection on

the history of surgery. (p116)

Writers' Museum All you ever wanted to know about Robert Burns, Walter Scott and Robert Louis Stevenson. (p40)

Best Museum Architecture

Scottish National Portrait Gallery Gorgeous palace in Venetian Gothic style, studded with sculptures of famous Scots. (p66)

National Museum of Scotland Staid Victorian building set off by flamboyant modern extension in golden sandstone. (p30)

Museum of Edinburgh Set in a 16th-century house with colourful, ornate decoration in red and yellow ochre. (p38)

Worth a Trip

The grounds of 19th-century Bonnington House, 10 miles west of Edinburgh, have been converted into a gorgeous sculpture park called **Jupiter Artland** (☎01506-889900; www.jupiterartland.org; Steadings, Wilkieston; adult/child £8.50/4.50; ⏱10am-5pm Thu-Sun late May–mid-Sep, daily Jul & Aug). It showcases works by a clutch of Britain's leading artists. First Edinburgh bus 27 or X27 departs every 30 minutes (hourly on Sunday) from stops on Princes St and Dalry Rd.

Best
Festivals & Events

Edinburgh is one of the biggest party venues in the world, with a crowded calendar of contrasting festivals, ranging from science and storytelling to music, movies and military bands. High season is August, when half a dozen festivals – including the huge Edinburgh International Festival, and the even bigger Festival Fringe – run concurrently. It's closely followed by the Christmas festival in December, which runs into the Hogmanay celebrations.

DOMINIAL_200S/SHUTTERSTOCK ©

Edinburgh International Festival

First held in 1947 to mark a return to peace after the ordeal of WWII, the Edinburgh International Festival is festooned with superlatives – the oldest, the biggest, the most famous, the best in the world. The festival takes place over the three weeks ending on the first Saturday in September; the program is usually available from April. Tickets sell out quickly, so it's best to book as far in advance as possible.

Edinburgh Festival Fringe

When the first Edinburgh International Festival was held in 1947, there were eight theatre companies that didn't make it onto the main program. Undeterred, they grouped together and held their own mini-festival, on the fringe, and an Edinburgh institution was born. The Fringe takes place over 3½ weeks, the last two overlapping with the first two of the Edinburgh International Festival.

Big-name tickets can cost £15 and up, but there are plenty of good shows in the £5 to £10 range and lots of free stuff. Fringe Sunday – usually the second Sunday – is a smorgasbord of free performances, staged in the Meadows park to the south of the city centre.

☑ **Top Tips**

▶ *The List* (www.list.co.uk) is a fortnightly events and listings magazine (also covering Glasgow), available from most newsagents. It has competition in the form of *The Skinny* (www.theskinny.co.uk), another listings mag covering both Edinburgh and Glasgow.

Best Festivals

Edinburgh International Science Festival
(☉April) Hosts a wide range of events, including talks, lectures, exhibitions, demonstrations, guided tours and interactive experiments designed to stimulate, inspire and challenge.

Edinburgh Christmas market, Princes Street Gardens (p68)

Imaginate Festival
(☺May) Britain's biggest festival of performing arts for children, with events suitable for kids aged three to 12 years. Groups from around the world perform classic tales like *Hansel and Gretel*, as well as new material written specially for children.

Edinburgh International Film Festival
(☺June) The two-week film festival is a major international event, serving as a showcase for new British and European films, and staging the European premieres of one or two Hollywood blockbusters.

Edinburgh International Festival
(☺August) Hundreds of the world's top musicians and performers congregate for three weeks of diverse and inspirational music, opera, theatre and dance.

Edinburgh Festival Fringe
(☺August) The biggest festival of the performing arts anywhere in the world.

Edinburgh Military Tattoo
(☺August) A spectacular display of military marching bands, massed pipes and drums, acrobats, cheerleaders and motorcycle display teams, all played out in front of the magnificent backdrop of the floodlit castle.

Edinburgh International Book Festival
(☺August) A fun fortnight of talks, readings, debates, lectures, book signings and meet-the-author events, with a cafe and tented bookshop thrown in.

Best Events

Beltane
(☺April) A pagan fire festival, resurrected in modern form, marking the end of winter, celebrated on the summit of Calton Hill. Held on the night of 30 April into the early hours of 1 May.

Royal Highland Show
(☺late June) A four-day feast of all things rural, from tractor driving to sheep shearing.

Edinburgh's Christmas
(☺December) Includes a street parade, fairground and Ferris wheel, and an open-air ice rink in Princes Street Gardens.

Edinburgh's Hogmanay
(☺From 29 December to 1 January) Events and include a torchlight procession and huge street party.

Best
Architecture

LONELY PL_NET/GETTY IMAGES ©

Edinburgh's unique beauty arises from a combination of its unusual site, perched among craggy hills, and a legacy of fine architecture dating from the 16th century to the present day. The New Town remains the world's most complete and unspoilt example of Georgian architecture and town planning. Along with the Old Town, it was declared a Unesco World Heritage Site in 1995.

Old Town Tenements

Edinburgh's Old Town features the biggest concentration of surviving 17th-century buildings in Britain. These tenements, six to eight storeys high, were among the tallest in Britain in their time. You can explore such tenements at Gladstone's Land (p38) and John Knox House (p40).

Georgian Gorgeousness

Robert Adam (1728–92), one of the leading architects of the Georgian period, made his mark in Edinburgh's New Town with neoclassical masterpieces such as Charlotte Sq (p75) and Edinburgh University's Old College. Experience the elegance of Adam's interiors by visiting the Georgian House (p75).

Modern Masterpiece

The plan for the New Town was the result of a competition won by James Craig, then an unknown, self-taught 23-year-old architect. At the end of the 20th century another architectural competition resulted in the relatively unknown Enric Miralles being chosen as the architect for the new Scottish Parliament Building (p56). Though its construction was controversial, the building won the 2005 Stirling Prize for the best new architecture in Britain, and has revitalised a near-derelict industrial site at the foot of the Royal Mile.

☑ **Top Tips**

▶ The website www. edinburgharchitecture.co.uk is crammed with useful info, including guided architectural walking tours.

Best Modern Architecture

Scottish Parliament Building Ambitious, controversial and way over budget; the most exciting example of modern architecture in Scotland. (p56)

National Museum of Scotland The museum's golden sandstone lines create echoes of castles, churches, gardens and cliffs. (p30)

Scottish Poetry Library Award-winning building, cleverly insinuated into a cramped space in an Old Town alley. (p44)

Front Range The designer glasshouses in Edinburgh's Royal Botanic Garden, built in 1967, are included in *Prospect* magazine's Top 100 Modern Scottish Buildings. (p96)

Best Neoclassical Architecture

Charlotte Square The elegantly proportioned Adam facade on the square's north side is the jewel in the New Town's architectural crown. (p75)

Royal Scottish Academy Recently stone-cleaned, this imposing William Playfair–designed Doric temple dominates the centre of Princes St. (p75)

Dundas House Gorgeous Palladian mansion that now houses a bank; pop into the main hall for a look at the dome, painted blue and studded with glazed stars. (p129)

Best Early Architecture

George Heriot's School Imposing renaissance building (1628–1650), funded by George Heriot (nicknamed Jinglin' Geordie), goldsmith and jeweller to King James VI. (p99)

Parliament Hall Dating from 1639, this grandiose hall has a majestic hammer-beam roof, and was home to the Scottish Parliament until the 1707 *Act of Union*. (p41)

Best Monuments

Scott Monument This Gothic space rocket parked amid the greenery of Princes Street Gardens celebrates Scotland's most famous historical novelist, Sir Walter Scott. (p69)

Nelson Monument Built in the shape of an upturned telescope, this slender tower on the summit of Calton Hill was built to commemorate Nelson's victory at Trafalgar in 1805. (p76)

Melville Monument Edinburgh's answer to London's Nelson's Column towers over St Andrew Sq, topped by a statue of Henry Dundas (1742–1811), the most powerful Scottish politician of his time. (p129)

National Monument An unfinished folly atop Calton Hill; its Greek temple–like appearance gave Edinburgh the nickname 'Athens of the North'. (p76)

Best Tours

Best Walking Tours

City of the Dead Tours
This tour of Greyfriars Kirkyard is probably the scariest of Edinburgh's 'ghost' tours. Many people have reported encounters with the McKenzie Poltergeist, the ghost of a 17th-century judge who persecuted the Covenanters, and now haunts their former prison in a corner of the kirkyard. Not suitable for young children. (www.cityofthedeadtours.com; adult/concession £10/8)

Edinburgh Literary Pub Tour
An enlightening, two-hour trawl through Edinburgh's literary history – and its associated howffs (meeting places, often pubs) – in the entertaining company of Messrs Clart and McBrain. (www.edinburghliterarypubtour.co.uk; adult/student £14/10; ⊘7.30pm daily May-Sep, limited days Oct-Apr)

Mercat Tours
Mercat offers a wide range of fascinating history walks and 'Ghosts & Ghouls' tours, but its most famous is a visit to the hidden, haunted, underground vaults beneath South Bridge (p35). (📞0131-225 5445; www.mercattours.com; Mercat Cross; adult/child £12/7)

Cadies & Witchery Tours
The becloaked and pasty-faced Adam Lyal (deceased) leads a Murder & Mystery tour of the Old Town's darker corners. These tours are famous for their 'jumper-ooters' – costumed actors who 'jump oot' when you least expect it. (📞0131-225 6745; www.witcherytours.com; adult/child £10/7.50)

Rebus Tours
A two-hour guided tour of the 'hidden Edinburgh' frequented by novelist Ian Rankin's fictional detective, John Rebus. Not recommended for children under 10. (📞0131-553 7473; www.rebustours.com; per

person £10; ⊘ noon Sat)

Best Bus Tours

Majestic Tour
Hop-on/hop-off tour departing every 15 to 20 minutes from Waverley Bridge to the Royal Yacht *Britannia* at Ocean Terminal via the New Town, Royal Botanic Garden and Newhaven, returning via Leith Walk, Holyrood and the Royal Mile. (www.edinburghtour.com; adult/child £15/7.50; ⊘ daily year-round)

MacTours
A quick tour around the highlights of the Old and New Towns, from the castle to Calton Hill, aboard an open-topped vintage bus. (www.edinburghtour.com; adult/child £15/7.50; ⊘ every 30 min Apr-Oct)

Survival Guide

→ **Tram** Edinburgh Trams (www.edinburghtrams.com) run from the airport to the city centre (one way/return £5.50/8.50, 33 minutes, every six to eight minutes from 6am to midnight).

→ **Taxi** An airport taxi to the city centre costs around £20 and takes about 20 to 30 minutes.

Edinburgh Waverley Train Station

→ The main train terminus in Edinburgh is Waverley train station, located in the heart of the city. Trains arriving from, and departing for, the west also stop at Haymarket station (Map p73, E4), which is more convenient for the West End.

Getting Around

Bus

→ The main bus operators are **Lothian Buses**

(☎0131-555 6363; www.lothianbuses.com) and **First** (www.firstgroup.com). For timetable information contact **Traveline** (☎0871 200 22 33; www.travelinescotland.com).

→ Bus timetables, route maps and fare guides are posted at all main bus and tram stops.

→ You can pick up a copy of the free *Lothian Buses Route Map* from Lothian Buses Travelshops.

→ Adult fares within the city are £1.60; purchase from the bus driver. Children aged under five years travel free and those aged five to 15 pay a flat fare of 80p.

→ Night-service buses (www.nightbuses.com) run hourly between midnight and 5am, and charge a flat fare of £3.50.

→ Lothian Bus drivers sell a day ticket (£4) that gives unlimited travel on Lothian buses and trams for a day; a family day ticket (up to two adults and three children) costs £8.50.

Tram

→ Edinburgh's tram line (www.edinburghtrams.com) runs from Edinburgh Airport to York Pl, at the top of Leith Walk, via Haymarket, the West End and Princes St.

→ Tickets are integrated with the city's Lothian Buses, costing £1.60 for a single journey within the city boundary, or £5.50 to the airport.

→ Trams run every eight to 10 minutes Monday to Saturday, and every 12 to 15 minutes on a Sunday, from 5.30am to 11pm.

Taxi

→ Edinburgh's black taxis can be hailed in the street, ordered by phone (extra 80p charge) or picked up at one of the many central ranks.

Central Taxis (☎0131-229 2468; www.taxis-edinburgh.co.uk)

City Cabs (☎0131-228 1211; www.citycabs.co.uk)

ComCab (☎0131-272 8001; www.comcab-edinburgh.co.uk)

→ The minimum fare is £2.10 (£3.10 at night) for the first 450m, then 25p for every subsequent 188m – a typical 2-mile trip across the city centre will cost around £6 to £7.

➡ Tipping is up to you – because of the high fares local people rarely tip on short journeys, but occasionally round up to the nearest 50p on longer ones.

Bicycle

➡ Edinburgh is well equipped with bike lanes and dedicated cycle tracks.

➡ You can buy a map of the city's cycle routes from most bike shops.

➡ **Biketrax** (Map p114; 📞0131-228 6633; www. biketrax.co.uk; 11-13 Lochrin Pl; per day from £17; 🕑9.30am-6pm Mon-Fri, to 5.30pm Sat, noon-5pm Sun; 🚌all Tollcross buses) rents out hybrid bikes, road bikes and Brompton folding bikes (no mountain bikes, though). You'll need a £100 cash or credit-card deposit and photographic ID.

Car & Motorcycle

➡ Though useful for day trips beyond the city, a car in central Edinburgh is more of a liability than a convenience; finding a parking spot in the city centre is like striking gold.

➡ All the big, international car-rental agencies have offices in Edinburgh, including **Avis** (Map p73, 1F; 📞0844 544 6059; www. avis.co.uk; 24 East London St; 🕑8am-6pm Mon-Fri, 8am-2pm Sat, 10am-2pm Sun) and **Europcar** (Map p73, 4F; 📞0871 384 3453; www. europcar.co.uk; Platform 2, Waverley Train Station, Waverley Bridge; 🕑7am-8pm Mon-Fri, 7am-5pm Sat & Sun).

➡ There are many smaller, local agencies that offer better rates. **Arnold Clark** (📞0141-237 4374; www.arnoldclarkrental. co.uk) charges from £32 a day, or £185 a week for a small car, including VAT and insurance.

Essential Information

Business Hours

Banks 9.30am-4pm Monday to Friday; some branches open 9.30am-1pm Saturday

Businesses 9am-5pm Monday to Friday

Pubs and bars 11am-11pm Monday to Thursday, 11am-1am Friday and Saturday, 12.30pm-11pm Sunday

Restaurants noon-2.30pm and 6-10pm

Shops 9am-5.30pm Monday to Saturday; some to 8pm Thursday; 11am-5pm Sunday

Discount Cards

➡ Royal Edinburgh Ticket includes admission to the Royal Yacht *Britannia*, Edinburgh Castle and the Palace of Holyroodhouse, plus unlimited travel on hop-on, hop-off tour buses among the various attractions.

Electricity

230V/50Hz

Emergency

In in emergency, dial ⏱999 or ⏱112 to call the police, ambulance, fire brigade or coastguard.

Money

Currency

➡ The unit of currency in the UK is the pound sterling (£).

➡ One pound sterling consists of 100 pence (called 'p' colloquially).

➡ Banknotes come in denominations of £5, £10, £20 and £50.

➡ Scottish banks issue their own banknotes, meaning there's quite a variety of different notes in circulation. They are harder to exchange outside the UK, so swap for Bank of England notes before you leave.

ATMs

➡ Automatic teller machines (ATMs – often called cashpoints) are widespread.

➡ You can use Visa, MasterCard, Amex, Cirrus, Plus and Maestro cards to withdraw cash from ATMs belonging to most banks and building societies.

➡ Cash withdrawals from non-bank ATMs, usually found in shops, may be subject to a charge of £1.50 or £2.

Credit Cards

➡ Visa and MasterCard are widely accepted, though some small businesses will charge for accepting them.

➡ Charge cards such as Amex and Diners Club are less widely used.

Money Changers

➡ The best-value place to change money is at post offices, where no commission is charged.

➡ Be careful using bureaux de change; they may offer good exchange rates but frequently levy outrageous commissions and fees.

Tipping

➡ **Hotels** One pound per bag is standard; gratuity for cleaning staff is completely at your discretion.

➡ **Pubs** Not expected unless table service is provided, then £1 for a round of drinks.

➡ **Restaurants** For decent service 10%, up to 15% at more expensive places. Check to see if service has been added to the bill already (most likely for large groups).

➡ **Taxis** Generally rounded up to nearest pound.

Public Holidays

➡ **New Year's Day** 1 January

➡ **New Year Bank Holiday** 2 January

➡ **Spring Bank Holiday** second Monday in April

➡ **Good Friday** Friday before Easter Sunday

➡ **Easter Monday** Monday following Easter Sunday

➡ **May Day** first Monday in May

➡ **Christmas Day** 25 December

➡ **Boxing Day** 26 December

Safe Travel

➡ Keep your passport, cash and credit cards separate.

➡ Edinburgh is a relatively safe city, so exercising common sense should keep you safe.

➡ Avoid crossing the Meadows (the park that lies between the Old own and Marchmont) lone after dark.

Telephone

→ There are plenty of public phones in Edinburgh, operated by either coins, phonecards or credit cards; phonecards are available in newsagents.

→ Edinburgh's area code is ☎0131, followed by a seven-digit number. You only need to dial the ☎0131 prefix when you are calling Edinburgh from outside the city, or if you're dialling from a mobile.

→ To call abroad from the UK, dial the international access code (☎00), then the area code (dropping any initial 0), followed by the telephone number.

Mobile Phones

→ The UK uses the GSM 900/1800 network, which is compatible with the rest of Europe, Australia and New Zealand, but not with the North American GSM 1900 system or Japanese mobile technology.

→ If in doubt, check with your service provider; some North American

operators have GSM 1900/900 phones that will work in the UK.

→ Edinburgh has excellent 3G coverage.

Phone Codes

International dialling code ☎00

Edinburgh area code ☎0131

Mobile phone numbers ☎07

Local call ☎0845; local call rates on UK landlines; 15p to 40p per minute from mobiles

National call ☎0870; national call rates on UK landlines; 15p to 40p per minute from mobiles

Premium call rate ☎09; £1.50 per minute

Toll-free numbers ☎0800 or 0808; from UK landlines; 15p to 30p per minute from mobiles

Useful Numbers

International directory enquiries ☎153

International operator ☎155

Local & national directory enquiries ☎118 500

Local & national operator ☎100

Reverse-charge/ collect calls ☎155

Speaking clock ☎123

Toilets

→ Public toilets are free to use and are spread across the city.

→ Most are open from 10am to 8pm.

→ Find the nearest one at www.edinburgh.gov.uk: search for 'public toilet'.

Tourist Information

Edinburgh Information Centre

(Map p73, E4; ☎0131-473 3868; www.edinburgh.org; Waverley Mall, 3 Princes St; ⏰9am-7pm Mon-Sat, 10am-7pm Sun Jul & Aug, to 6pm Jun, to 5pm Sep-May; 🛜; 🚇St Andrew Sq) Has an accommodation booking service, currency exchange, gift and bookshop, internet access and counters selling tickets for Edinburgh city tours and Scottish Citylink bus services.

Edinburgh Airport Information Centre

(☎0131-473 3690; www.edinburghairport.com; Edinburgh Airport; ⏰7.30am-7.30pm Mon-Fri, to 8pm Sat & Sun) VisitScotland

Information Centre in the airport's terminal extension.

Travellers with Disablities

➡ Download Lonely Planet's free Accessible Travel guide from http://lptravel.to/Accessible-Travel

➡ Edinburgh's Old Town, with its steep hills, narrow closes, flights of stairs and cobbled streets, is a challenge for wheelchair users.

➡ Large new hotels and modern tourist attractions are usually fine; however, many B&Bs and guesthouses are in hard-to-adapt, older buildings that lack ramps and lifts.

➡ Newer buses have steps or kneeling suspension that lowers for access, but it's wise to check before setting out. Most black taxis are wheelchair-friendly.

➡ Many banks are fitted with induction loops to assist the hearing impaired.

➡ Some attractions have Braille guides for the visually impaired.

➡ VisitScotland (www.visitscotland.com) has an online guide to accessible accommodation for travellers with disabilities.

Visas

➡ If you're a citizen of the EEA (European Economic Area) nations or Switzerland, you don't need a visa to enter or work in Britain. However visa regulations are always subject to change, especially likely in light of Britain's 2016 EU referendum result, so it's essential to check before leaving home.

➡ Currently, if you're a citizen of Australia, Canada, New Zealand, Japan, Israel, the US and several other countries, you can stay for up to six months (no visa required), but are not allowed to work.

➡ Nationals of other countries, including South Africa, will need to obtain a visa: for more info, see www.ukvisas.gov.uk.

Behind the Scenes

Send Us Your Feedback

We love to hear from travellers – your comments help make our books better. We read every word, and we guarantee that your feedback goes straight to the authors. Visit **lonelyplanet.com/contact** to submit your updates and suggestions.

Note: We may edit, reproduce and incorporate your comments in Lonely Planet products such as guidebooks, websites and digital products, so let us know if you don't want your comments reproduced or your name acknowledged. For a copy of our privacy policy visit lonelyplanet.com/privacy

Our Readers

Many thanks to the travellers who used the last edition and wrote to us with helpful hints, useful advice and interesting anecdotes:

Caroline Mundye, Graham Price, Lourdes Capó, Ludovica Moro, Luisa Méndez.

Acknowledgements

Cover photograph: Calton Hill and view towards Princes Street; Maurizio Rellini/4Corners©

This Book

This 4th edition of Lonely Planet's *Pocket Edinburgh* guidebook was researched and written by Neil Wilson. The previous two editions were also written by Neil Wilson. This guidebook was produced by the following:

Destination Editor
James Smart

Product Editor
Jessica Ryan, Catherine Naghten

Senior Cartographers
Alison Lyall, Mark Griffiths

Book Designer
Gwen Cotter

Assisting Editors
Gabby Innes, Lauren O'Connell, Fionnuala Twomey, Simon Williamson

Cover Researcher
Naomi Parker

Thanks to
Cheree Broughton, Daniel Corbett, Claire Naylor, Karyn Noble, Angela Tinson, Lauren Wellicome, Tony Wheeler

Index

See also separate subindexes for:

Eating p157
Drinking p157
Entertainment p158
Shopping p158

Sights 000
Map Pages **000**

Our Writer

Neil Wilson

Neil was born in Scotland and has lived there most of his life. Based in Perthshire, he has been a full-time writer since 1988, working on more than 80 guidebooks for various publishers, including the Lonely Planet guides to Scotland, England, Ireland and Prague. An outdoors enthusiast since childhood, Neil is an active hill-walker, mountain-biker, sailor, snowboarder, fly-fisher and rock-climber, and has climbed and tramped in four continents, including ascents of Jebel Toubkal in Morocco, Mount Kinabalu in Borneo, the Old Man of Hoy in Scotland's Orkney Islands and the Northwest Face of Half Dome in California's Yosemite Valley.

Published by Lonely Planet Global Limited
CRN 554153
4th edition – Apr 2017
ISBN 978 1 78657 331 5
© Lonely Planet 2017   Photographs © as indicated 2017
10 9 8 7 6 5 4 3
Printed in China